BIBLE RECORDS
Vol. I
Barbour County, Alabama

Compiled by
Helen S. Foley

Southern Historical Press, Inc.
Greenville, South Carolina

Copyright 1976
By: Helen S. Foley

Copyright Transferred 1983
To: Southern Historical Press, Inc.

All rights reserved. No part of this publication may be reproduced, stored in a retrieval system, transmitted in any form, posted on to the web in any form or by any means without the prior written permission of the publisher.

Please direct all correspondence and orders to:

www.southernhistoricalpress.com
or
SOUTHERN HISTORICAL PRESS, Inc.
PO BOX 1267
375 West Broad Street
Greenville, SC   29601
southernhistoricalpress@gmail.com

ISBN #0-89308-180-9

Printed in the United States of America

Foreword

The Bible Records in this book were copied from the originals and no records were changed. Only two corrections were made and these will be found in the footnotes. These records, with the exception of a very small number, pertain to families who are living or who once lived in Barbour County, Alabama and the adjoining areas. Many of these Bible are still owned by residents of this county and surrounding counties.

Barbour County was formed from the Cession of 1812 and from parts of Henry and Pike Counties in the year of 1832. It was named for James Barbour, of Virginia.

ADAMS Bible

FAMILY REGISTER of Jonathan Adams
The Grand parents of Jonathan Adams

James Adams was born A.D. 1733.
Mary Adams, his wife was born the 16 of May 1743.
David Adams, father of Jonathan Adams, was born 28 January 1766 - died 19 Octob. 1834.
Betsy Adams, Mother of Jonathan Adams, was born the 16 of Aug. 1779 died in the summer of 18-- (illegible).
Jonathan Adams was born in Hancock County Georgia the 11 of October 1803.
Mary Adams Wife of Jonathan was born in Green County, Ga. February 11, 1812.
Jonathan Adams & Mary Gray were married in Upson County Georgia on the 3 of April 1829.

The children of Jonathan & Mary Adams:
  David Adams was born June the 1st 1831; died the 16 April 1834.
  Archibald G. Adams was born 4th of July 1833 in Zebulon.
  David Brasfield Adams was born 29 of July 1835 in Zebulon, died 17 June 1862.
  Martha Caroline Adams was born the 26 of March 1837.
  Cinthia Elisabeth was born 27 of August 1840.
  Rebecca Jane Adams was born 28 July 1842.
  Georgia Anna Texas was born April 27th 1845.
  John Epinger Adams was born 10th January 1848.
  Jefferson Montgomery Adams was born the 10 of Januy in Meriweather Co. Georgia 1849.

A. C. Powell & Elizabeth Adams were married in Harrison County Texas January 5th 1870.
David Brasfield Adams died in the army at Enterprise Mississippi the 17 of June 1862.
Dr. Jonathan Adams died the 15th of June 1864.
Georgia A. Powell Departed this Life on 26th of March 1868 Age 22 years and Eleven months.
Mary Adams wife of Dr. Jonathan Adams died on the 27th of April 1870 at 10 minutes to 5 o.c. A. M.
S. H. Powell and R. J. Adams was married 23d of December 1869.
Archibald G. Adams & Johnnie Smith was married the 18th of March 1868 at Jefferson, Marion Co., Tex.
Jefferson Montgomery Adams & Mary Ollie McReynolds were married in Cass County Texas Thursday, February 5th, 1874.
Archibald Brasfield Son of Jefferson & Ollie Adams was born July 10th 1877.
Archibald Gray Adams & Kate Edwina Wilson were married Dec. 16th 1903 - at Comanche Texas.
Archibald Gray Adams & Lucile Richardson were married July 1st 1935 Texas
Josephine Georgia Adams the daughter of Archibald & Johnie Adams was born the 15 Sept. 1872.
Elizabeth Haynes Adams daughter of A. G. Adams & Johnnie was born Nov. 10th 1874.

ADAMS Bible, cont.
Archibald Gray Adams, Jr. son of Archie & Johnnie Adams was
    born Aug. 31 1876.
Archibald Gray Adams son of A. G., Jr. and Kate Adams was born
    July 17th 1906.
Frank Wilson Adams son of Archibald Gray Adams & Kate E. Adams
    was born Marshall Texas Oct. 2, 1912.
Robt. Marshall Adams - son of Archibald Gray & Kate E. Adams
    was born in Jacksonville Texas A   6th 19--.
Mary Katharine Adams daughter of Archibald Gray Adams & Kate E.
    Adams was born Jacksonville Texas Aug. 21 19--.
Alice Elina Adams - daughter of Archibald Gray Adams and
    Lucille Adams was born June 17th 194-.
Archibald Gray Adams Sr. died Sept 3rd 1915.
Johnie E. Adams, wife of Archibald G. Adams Sr. died March
    27th 1927.
Archibald Gray Adams 2nd born Aug. 31st 1876 died June 16 1948.
David Adams Sr. died in Zebulon the 16 of April 1834.

(The following not included in ADAMS Bible Records - sent as
an exact copy of the inscription on the monument).

ADAMS Cemetery in Jasper Co., Ga.
Sacred to the Memory of General David Adams who died October
    19, 1834, in the 69th year of his age.

Near him are buried his Daughter, Mary, his Mother and two
    Brothers, Jonathan and James Adams.

General Adams was a native of South Carolina and came to the
State of Georgia soon after the Revolution of 1776. He was
a Member of The Legislature more than 20 years, and at different
times presided as Speaker of the House of Representatives. He
received successively from the State the Commission of Brigadier
and Major General.

WOOD Bible

Filed in the Department of Archives and History, Montgomery,
Alabama.

MARRIAGES:
Young Wood the son of Furnifold Wood and Abigail Wood his wife
    was bournd the 22 day of September 1794 in Sampson County
    North Carolina.
Rosanna Byrd Daughter of Rich. Byrd and Jean Byrd his wife was
    bournd the 27 day of September 1802 in Lenoir County North
    Carolina.
Young Wood and Rosanna Wood his wife was Married the 22 day of
    December 1825 in Wayne County North Carolina.
John R. Wood the son of the above parents was bourned the 9
    day of Novr. 1827 in Wayne Co., N. C.
Nancy Ann Wood daughter of the above parents was bournd the 5 da
    of January 1829 in Wayne County North Carolina.
Green Wood the son of the above parents was bourned the 22 day
    of April 1830 in Wayne County North Carolina.
William D. Wood the Son of the above parents was bournd the

22 day of Septr. 1835 in Barbour County Alabama
George W. Searcy and Nancy Ann Wood were married in George-
   town, Ga. (Note: date not given).
E. F. Davis of Laurenceville Ala. and Mary Ann Searcy were
   married May 10, 1868 by John J. Cassady.
Fred Bacon Cullens and Annie Laurie Davis were married in Ozark,
   Ala. Sep. 17, 1890.
Lovick W. Philips and George Searcy Davis were married in
   Ozark, Ala. by Rev. Hurley.
Elnathan Davis II married Mrs. ---sia Brunson Byrd Oct. 1933.
Mary Florine Davis Married Ben Posey, N. Carolina, Jan. 1909.
Lovick W. Philips married Mabel ------------Aug. 1929.
Abram Lewis Philips married Mary Rice March 1935.
Helen Davis Cullens married William James Carter, 1941.

BIRTHS:
Elnathan Franklin Davis, Oct. 5, 1835, Henry Co., Ga. near Griffin.
Mary Annie Searcy, Henry Co., Ala., March 5, 1851.
Minnie May Davis, Feb. 20, 1869, Lawrenceville, Ala.
James Jefferson Davis, Jan. 6, 1871, Lawrenceville, Ala.
Annie Laurie Davis, Feb. 14, 1873, Lawrenceville, Ala.
Alberta Clyde Davis, Feb. 26, 1875,   "   "
George Searcy Davis, Feb. 16, 1878,   "   "
Mary Florine Davis, Dec. 16, 1880, Eufaula, Ala.
Emma Lydia Davis, July 2, 1883, Eufaula, Ala.
Elnathan Franklin Davis, June 15, 1891, Ozark, Ala.
Frederick Bacon Cullens, Jr., Oct. 4, 1891, Ozark, Ala.
Annie Laurie Cullens, May 30, 1893, Ozark, Ala.
James Wimberly Cullens, Aug. 4, 1895, "   "
John Frances Cullens, Nov. 2, 1897,   "   "
Mary Emma Cullens, April 11, 1903,   "   "
Helen Cullens, (Note: No date).   "   "
Lovick Wynton Philips, Russell Co., Ala. (No date).
Georgie Bert Phillips,   "   "   "   "   "
James Franklin Philips,   "   "   "   "   "
Abram Lewis Philips, 1st, Oct. 1, 1908, Columbus, Ga.
Abram Lewis Philips, IInd, 1935, Columbus, Ga.
John Davis Philips, Sept. 1942
Helen Cullens Carter, 1941
Nancy Wimberly Carter, 1943.
Jack Cullens, Jr., Oct. 1944.

DEATHS:
Young Wood, County Line (Note: No date. County Line Cemetery is
   in Henry Co., Ala., on the Barbour Co., line).
Rosanna Wood, County Line
George W. Searcy Apr. 26, 1880, Henry Co., Ala., buried at
   County Line.
Nancy Ann Searcy, July 4, 1905, Henry Co., Ala., buried at
   County Line.
E. Frank Davis, Sept. 15, 1906, Montgomery, Ala., 12 Noble Ave.
Alberta Clyde Davis, Montgomery, Apr. 29, 1925.
James Jefferson Davis, June 19, 1928.
Mary Ann Davis, Dec. 1929.
Georgia Searcy Philips, Jan. 1931.
(Continued).

WOOD Bible continued:
Florine Davis Posey, Oct. 1938
Georgia Bert Philips, Oct. 1942
Girl baby of L. W. and Georgie Philips, Russell Co., Ala.(No dat
James Franklin Philips, Russell Co., (Ala.) (No date).

RICHARDS - CARTER Bible of Barbour County, Alabama
MARRIAGES:
This Certified That the Rite of Holy Matrimony was Celebrated Between Thomas Richards of Henry County, Ala., and Lucy Carter of Barbour County, Ala. on 22d Augt. 1826 at Esqr. Deal's house by Lewis Deal, Esqr. Witnesses: Energy E. Black - Flora McLean

Thomas Benton Richards & Clee R. Wheeler were married by Rev.
    Cato Parker Janry 17th 1865
Alonzo Lucratus Richards & Abigail R. Wood were Married by
    Rev'd Moses Helms Dec. 15th 1881

BIRTHS:
Thos. Richards born Septr. 14th 1798.
Lucy Carter born May 10th 1806.
Robert Carter born March 2d, 1820.
Andrew Jackson Richards born Augt. 7th 1827.
Sonia Jane Richards born Augt. 16th 1828
Benj. Franklin Richards born June 7th 1830.
Robert Emet Richards born Nov. 18th 1831.
Giles Washington Richards born June 1st 1833
Thos. Benton Richards born July 31, 1836
Seaborn Lafayett Richards born Janry 6th 1839.
William Wesley Richards born Bebry 28 1841.
Lucy Ann Richards born Janry 19, 1845.
Joseph Lafayett Richards born March 28, 1847
Alonozo Locratous Richards born April 28 1849.
Fanny Richards born July 11 1851.
Thos. Hinton Richards born Septr. 5, 1857
Thos. A. Richards, born Oct. 24th 1882.
Frankie V. Richards born July 21 1884
Lucy P. Richards born Oct. 20th 1885
Helen A. Richards born June 18th 1887
Eva Richards born Jan. 29th 1889.
Rubie Richards born July 17th 1890
Ben L. Richards born 1st 1895.

DEATHS:
Catherine Carter departed this life Novr. 20th 1829.
Seaborn Lafayett Richards departed this life May 1st 1840.
Elizabeth Hendrick departed this life Septr. 2 1843.
Ellen Richards departed this life Septr. 28 1848
Fanny Richards departed this life Augt. 7 1851.
Robert Richards departed this life July 18 1851
Mary Pinson departed this life Sept. 17, 1852
N. A. Pitman departed this life Jany. 30 1855
Sonia Jane Hardwick departed this life Septr. 2d, 1857.
Rounda Richards departed this life Septr. 16 1857.
Joseph Lafayett Richards departed this life Febry 22, 1857.
(Continued).

Benj. F. Richards - Killed at Battle of Iuka
   Septr. 15, 1862.

Robert Emmet Richards died in Hospital Richmond Va. Jany 5, 1863.
Alice Carter departed this life (Note: Incomplete).
Giles Carter Departed this life Febry 27, 1864.
Thomas Richards departed this life June 23rd 1879.
Lucy A. Richards departed this life Septr. 14th 1890.
Ruby Richards departed this life Oct. 24th 1891.

WOOD Bible

MARRIAGES:
A. H. Wood and Margaret V. Morris January 7th 1855.
Jas. A. Wood and Fannie A. McLeroy Jan. 2nd 1878.
J. D. Wood and Mattie E. Vining March 2nd 1884.
Thomas D. Wood and Clara Bell Fields June 15, 1913.
Elmer E. Cargill and Mary H. Wood Oct. 22, 1912.
J. M. Cade & W. D. Wood June 6, 1913.
D. J. Vickery and Laura A. Wood January the 29th 1874.
J. T. Tye and Carrie L. Wood Nov. the 12th 1888.
J. D. Wood and Mrs. A. C. Kissington August 23, 1891.
B. F. Cockran and Ada P. Wood Nov. 29th 1891.
B. L. Bland & Margaret V. Wood Jan. 1916.
B. M. Turnipseed & A. E. Wood June 1920.
T. D. Wood & Ethel Chambliss (Chambers?) March 4, 1919.

BIRTHS:
A. H. Wood born Nov. 17th 1831.
Sonnorah Athens Wood was born April 19th, 1856.
Jacob Marshall Wood was born July 1st, 1859.
John M. Wood was born January 12th, 1864.
Robert Lee Wood was born Sept. 20th, 1870.
Margret V. Morris was born July 9th 1833.
James A. Wood was born December 28th, 1857.
Jefferson Davis Wood was born October 27th 1861.
Carrie Lou Wood was born August 3rd 1865.
Ada Pauline Wood was born Feb. 21st 18-- (last of date erased).
Andrew Jackson Vickery was born Jan. the 1st 1876.
Crawford R.(?) Wood was born February the 12, 1888.
Oceola Tye was born Oct. the 1st, 1884.
Morris Ryder Tye was born May the 28th 1888.
Thomas Dawson Wood was born Sept. 7th 1892.
Robert Franklin Wood was born the 27th Jan. 1900.
Addie Elizabeth was Born the 16 Day of Feb. 1902.
Etta Eliza Athens Vickery was born the 13th of Jan. 1878.
Una Vasti Wood was born December 14th 1885.
Jas H. Tye was born Jan the 7th 1886.
Fannie A. T. Tye was born the 8th of Dc. 1888.
Mary Hellin Wood was born Feb. 7th 1894.
Winie Davis Wood was born the 8 of Nov. 1895.
Margret Vastie Wood was born the 16th March 1898.

DEATHS:
A. H. Wood Died April the 39th 89.
M. V. Wood Died June 11th 1891.
(cont.)

J. D. Wood died June 27, 1920.
Addie C. Wood died April 27, 1921.
Matty Roberta Wood Died Feb. 26, 1889.
Una Vasti Wood Died Jan. 13, 1888.
Robert Franklin Wood Died Jan. 8th, 1900.
Johnie Marshall Wood was born Nov. 28, 1901, Died Oct. 13th 1901
    (Note: This is the way it is written in the Bible).
Infant child of Mr. & Mrs J. D. Wood was born & died Dec. 5, 1906.

McLEOD Bible
Owned by Mrs W. W. Stanton, Sylacauga, Ala.

MARRIAGES:
William (E.) McLeod was married to Nancy Ann Johnson the 30 day of
    September 1856.
(Illegible - other records indicate it should read James Silvester
    Watson) and Mary Lenora McLeod were married the 27 day of
    December 1877.
J. W. King was married to Leona McLeod Dec. 23, 1887.
W. F. Rose was married to Marion McLeod May 30th 1893.

BIRTHS:
Children of Wm. E. McLeod and Nancy Ann Johnson McLeod:
Mary Lenora (McLeod) was born August the 10 day 1857.
James Coleman (McLeod) was born October the 10 day 1859.
Alice Adella (McLeod) was bornd Febuary 7, 1862.
Sarah Elizabeth (McLeod) was borned Feby the 10 A.D. 1866.
Leona Christian (McLeod) was borned June the 28 AD. 1868.
Marion (McLeod) was born 2 day October 1870.
Willa Anna McLeod was Borned January the 8 day A.D. 1873.
Ruby Celistial (Celestia) McLeod was borned Nov. 14 A.D. 1875.
Elle Ree McLeod was borned (illegible).
Rosa Louise (McLeod) 18 day Dec. 1879.
Kathren McLeod 27 day Mar. 1882.
Papa born Aug. 10, 1830 (Wm. E. McLeod *).
Mamma born July 28, 1838 (Nancy Ann Johnson McLeod).

MARRIAGES:
James Silvester Watson & Mary Lenora McLeod married Dec. 27, 1877.
J. W. King & Leona (McLeod) Dec. 3, 1886.
W. F. Rose & Kittie Mae (Marion McLeod) May 30, 1893.
J. E. Howell & Alice (McLeod) Feb. 21, 1894.
R. E. Calhoun and Willie (McLeod) Jan. 29, 1900.
C. C. Davis & Rosa (McLeod) Dec. 3, 1902.
Jim Grubs and Alice H. (Howell) Dec. 28, 1902.
Robert Dunbar & Ruby (McLeod) ----------.

DEATHS:
Nancy Ann McLeod died July 29, 1892.
James Watson died Oct. 13, 1895.
James Coleman McLeod Aug. 10, 1900.
William McLeod Sept. 8, 1907.
(Cont.)

* Birth date entered in error - should have been 1825.

Marion McLeod Rose (died) Feb. 27, 1917.
Nora McLeod Watson (died) Nov. 8, 1937.
Rosa McLeod Davis (died) April 25, 1945.
Sallie McLeod (died) July 4, 1947.
Leona McLeod King (died) March 11, 1951.
Alice McLeod Grubbs died April 24, 1952.
Ruby McLeod Dunbar died Nov. 18, 1952.

BAXTER Bible
Owned by Victoria Baxter Lunsford, Barbour County, Ala.

BIRTHS:
Daniel T. Baxter was born near Louisville, Barbour County,
   Alabama July 20th 1848.
Elizabeth L. McRae was born Dec. 16, 1878.
Victoria Jones was born near Louisville, Barbour County,
   Alabama August 26th 1854.
Amanda Baxter was born March 3d, 1881.
Alice Greer Baxter was born June 19th 1884.
Charlie Baxter was born June the 6th 1886.
Dorathy Annelle Baxter was born Oct. 4th 1917.
Vera Elizabeth McRae Baxter was born Dec. 12, 1898.
Geraldine Baxter was born Oct. 1st, 1920.
Robert Olin Baxter was born July 16th 1926 Thursday.
Barbara Dean Young was born April 25, 1941.
Charles Marvin Grabin was born July 19, 1942 (Sun.)
Carla Gene Mann was born Thurs. April 9, 1943, weight 2 lb. 5 oz.
Robert Winfield Young, Jr. was born Oct. 7th 1944 (Sat.)
Peggy Diane Baxter was born Aug. 6th, 1950 (Sun.)
John Robert Baxter was born Oct. 26, 1955 (Wed.)
Charles David Lunsford was born Feb. 13, 1959 (Fri.)
Victoria Baxter born 26 Jan. 1922.

MARRIAGES:
Daniel T. Baxter & Victoria Jones, at the residence of Mathew
   Jones on the Eighteenth day of December in the year of our
   Lord One thousand eight hundred and Seventy Nine, State of
   Alabama.

DEATHS:
Alice Greer Baxter died January 6th 1885.
Victoria Baxter wife of Daniel T. Baxter departed this life
   October the 27th 1893.
Agusta Baxter wife of Daniel T. Baxter Departed this life
   January the 12th, 1909.
Daniel T. Baxter Departed this life May the 19, 1913.
Amanda (?) Baxter Norton Departed this life December 26, 1926.
William Walter McRae died Aug. 19, 1944, age 71.
Elizabeth Lunsford McRae died Aug 13, 1948, age 69.
Charlie H. Baxter died Aug. 21, 1951.

BARLOW - ALLDAY Bible
Owned by Mrs. O. D. Hooper, Eufaula, Ala.

MARRIAGES:
John Barlow was married to Elizabeth Johnson August 29th 1827.
(Continued)

William Allday was born the 1st of November 1803.
William Allday and Mary Crocker was married the 20" of Jan. 1824
Jno. C. Thomas and Martha M. A. Virginia Allday were married
    Tuesday 8:30 P.M. June 9th 1863.
Wilson Johnson was married Nov. the 8th 1829 to Nicy Alday.
Mary Crocker was Born the 23" of July 1807.
F. J. Allday & Sarah T. Taylor was married July 27, 1856.
Sarah Barlow daughter of Edmund Barlow born July 8th 1782.

BIRTHS:
Julia Ann Barlow was born May the 26th 1828.
Mary Ann Barlow was born Nov. the 10th, 1829.
Clarkey Ann Hall Barlow was born Jany the 8th 1831.
John Williamson Barlow was born Sept. the 20th 1832
Rebecca Allday was Born the 18" of September 1826.
John R. Allday was born the 19" of Jun 1830
John Barlow was born July the 7th 1807.
Elizabeth Johnson wife of John Barlow was born June 22nd 1805.
Benjamin C. F. Allday was born the December 25", 1832.
Fedrick I. Allday was born the 10" of January 1835.
Nancy A. H. Allday was born the 14" of October 1837.
Sarah Ann Elizabeth Allday was born the 16" of July 1840.
Hugh Lawson Irwin Johnson was born Oct. the 18th, 1830.
Mary Ann Elizabeth Johnson was born May the 8th, 1832.
George Smith Allday was born the 23" of February 1844.
Martha Melisa Ann Virginia Allday was Born on the 23rd of
    February 1845.
Samuel Greene Rutherford Wiggins was born on the 7 day of
    September 1847.
Wilson Johnson was born Oct. the 12, 1808.
Nicy Alday wife of Wilson Johnson was born April 18, 1809.
Mattie Croker daughter of John C. and Mattie V. Thomas was born
    June 23rd, 1865. Friday 2:30 P.M.
Annie Virginia Thomas daughter of J. C. & M. V. Thomas was borne
    Nov. 12th 1867 - 5 A.M.
John Curtis Thomas Feby. 27, 1842.
Edith Curtis, daughter of J. C. & M. V. Thomas born March
    15th 1871 Wednesday 5:30 P.M.
John Cortez Thomas March 3d, 1874, Tuesday.

DEATHS:
Julia Ann Barlow departed this life Oct. 21, 1829.
G. Rebecca Allday departed this life the 18" of September 1829.
John R. Allday departed this life July 23", 1832.
George L. Allday departed this life the 24" February 1844.
Wm. Alday departed this life November the 2th, 1854.
John Croker departed this life December 27th, 1855.
Hugh Lawson Irwin Johnson departed this life July the 7th, 1832.
Green W. Allday departed this life March 1st, 1866, aged 18 year
    5 months, 25 days.
Mary Allday March 10, 1875.
Edith Curtis Thomas died Sunday June 2nd 1878.
Arthur Morse Thomas died Monday Dec. 21st, 1878.
Nelly Thomas Monday June 30th 1879.
Agatha Tully wed. Feb. 8, 1886.

EFURD Bible
Records in the possession of Mrs. Marie Godfrey, Eufaula, Ala.

BIRTHS:
John T. Lewis was Borne the 5th of May 18--.
Thomas C. Efurd was borne January 14, 1800.
Polly Efurd My Wife was borne the 24 Day of May 1805.
John A. Efurd was borne the 18 Febuary 1822.
Lucyann Efurd was Borne Febuary the 3, 1824.
Wm. T. I. C. Efurd was Borne November 27th 1826.
Saryann L.(?) Efurd was Borne June 1th 1828.
Thomas C. Efurd was Borne December 27th 1830.
Mary L. Efurd was Borne November 27th 1833.
Giles C. Efurd was Borne November 18th 1836.
Julyann Efurd was Borne June 28th 1839.
Cornelius O. Martin was Borne November 9th 1819 (?).
Mary A. Cole was Borne April 27th 1828.
Sarah A. Cole was Borne December 20th 1830.
William O. Martin was Borne January 28th 1822.
Mary Martin was Born December 27th 1792.
Sophia Martin was Borne October 31th 1812.

MARRIAGES:
Thomas C. Efurd & Polly Johnson November 30th 1820.
Daniel G. Lewis & Lucyann Efurd Oct. 5th 1843.
J. A. Efurd and Mary Cope was married the 12 of September 1844.
31 January 1854 Tandy King and Mary Louise Efurd was married.
T. C. Efurd and E. C. Herring was married December 27th 1855.
G. C. Efurd and P. E. Johns was married Oct. 25 1860.

WILLIAM W. JOHNSON Bible
Published by M. Carey & Son, Philadelphia - 1817.
Owned by Miss Sarah H. Johnson, Troy, Alabama.

MARRIAGES:
William W. Johnson boarn 20th Octobr 1828.
Eli Harrod and Nancey Johnson was married the 23 of Aug. 1829.
Martha Ann Harrod was born 24 May 183?
Lewis A. T. Johnson and Patience E. Norton was married Dec. 3, 1837.
Alexander Johnson and Elizabeth Colins was married the 19 of
    December in the 1838.

BIRTHS:
Nancy Johnson born February 25th 1808.
Rachal Johnson born October 24th 1809.
Lucinda Johnson born April 30th 1811.
Barshaba Johnson born February 9th 1813.
Alexander Johnson born October 24th 1814.
Lewis Johnson born March 23th 1817.
Barshaba Johnson born December 27th 1818. (Note: Duplicate ?).
Minna Johnson born October 22nd 1820.
Felder B. Johnson born September the 13th 1823.
Manday Johnson born June 1th 1841.
Wilson Johnson born September 1th 18??
Marthay Johnson born Febuary 15th 184?
(Continued).

Sarah Johnson born June 14, 1793.
Mary Johnson born March 7th 1795.
Alexander Johnson born May 13 1797.
Elizabeth Johnson born March 7th 1799.
Thomas Johnston born January 21st, 1801.
Jesse Johnson born June 11th 1806.
DEATHS:
Eliasher Johnston Decd on the Eleventh of July in the year of
    our Lord 1824.
Stephen Johnson Died 20 August in the evening in the year 1836.
Rosanah Johnson died the 18 of January in the year 1837.
Elizabeth (?) Johnson Departed this life the 23 December 1857.
Alexander Johnson Departed this life Oct. 15 A.D. 1891.
            Graham
Nancy Williams #   was born the 30 of Jny 1756.
Stephen Johnson was born the 11th of November 1766
Rosanah Johnson was born 17th Jnry 1785
Nancy Williams departed this life 11th of April A.D. 1829

JOHNSON, FELDER B. (Benjah) Bible
Owned by Louie Blackmon, Troy, Ala. (Note: This Johnson family
    was related to the William W. Johnsons whose records
    precede these).

MARRIAGES:
Felder B. Johnson & Julian (Julia) Johnson was married
    January 29 1843.
D. Gillis and Mary E. Johnson was married April 14th 1867.
(Note: The next six entries had been marked through).
Felder B. Johnson (rest illegible).
Julia Johnson was bornd   the 6, 1824.
Martha Ann Johnson was bornd No. the 16 1845 (or 1843).
William Henry Johnson was bornd March the 24 1846.
Mary Elisabeth was bornd May the 16 1847.
Marget Rosaner was born Sept the 18 1848.

BIRTHS:
F. B. Johnson was borned Sept. 13, 1823.
Martha An Johnson was born No 16 1843 (or 1845) (Duplicate).
William Henry bornd March the 24th 1845.
Mary Elizabeth bornd May the 16 1846.
Marget Rosaner bornd September the 18 1847.
Nancey Lucindey was born March 28 1848.
Juley Frances was bornd October the 19 1850.
Rachel Ann Marindy was born May the 5 1852.
Lewis Alexander was Born Jan the 11 (or 17) 1845.
S. (or L.) Rebeckca Johnson was born Dec. the 24 1855.
Felder Bena J (Benjah) Johnson was born No the 22 1857.
Elijah L. Johnson was born the 25 June 1869 (changed to 1859).
T. A. Johnson was Born No the 30 1860 (changed to 1861).
James F. Johnson was born July 31st 1867.

BIRTHS:
Mary Elizabeth Gillis born January 20th 1868 3½ o'clock AM
(Continued).

DEATHS:
Lewis Alexander Johnson Died June the 9 1855.
James Fletcher Johnson Died Sept. the 26 1869.
Martha A. More Died November the 5 1871.
Elijah L. Johnson was deceased July the 15 1878.
F. A. Johnson departed this life January the 3 1902.
Felder B. Johnson died May 13, 1916.
Julia A. Johnson died Jan. 3, 1902.
Larer Ellis Deide the 25 of April 1856.
William Henry Johnson Died Dec. 16th 1911.
Rosa D. Killingworth died Feb. 16th 1931.

ALSTON Bible

Records in the possession of Mrs. S. E. Godfrey, Jr.
Eufaula, Alabama.

Jacob Dantzler, Sr., born South Carolina, 28th Sept. AD 1772 died 28th Aug. 1812 AD.
William Ott, b. Oct. 28, 1789 - D. June 26, 1857, buried in Miller Grave Yard 5 miles west of Clayton (Note: Ala.), married Mrs. Catherine Dantzler on the 13th of June 1813.
Jacob M. Dantzler, Jr., son of Jacob Dantzler, born Nov. 11th 1804.
John S. Dantzler, son of Jacob Dantzler, born May 16th 1803, died Sept. 16th 1817.
David A. Dantzler, son of Jacob Dantzler, born in South Carolina on Jan. 10th 1810, drowned in Tyger River, S. C. June 27 1829.
William S. Dantzler, son of Jacob Dantzler, born in South Carolina on Oct. 21st, 1811, died Aug. 15th 1812.
Edward S. Ott, son of Wm. Ott, born in S. C. Jan 1st, 1815, died April 18--.
Edward S. Ott, son of William & Catherine Ott, and Amanda Alston, daughter of William H. Alston were married in Columbus, Ga. Jul. 29, 1846.
Mary M. Ott, daughter of William Ott, was born 12th Dec. 1816.
Ann C. Ott, daughter of William Ott, was born 4th of March 1819.
Margaret A. Ott, daughter of William Ott, was born 23rd Sept. 1821.
Adarana Ott, daughter of William Ott, was born 10th Oct. 1823.
Anna M. Ott, daughter of Edward S. Ott, was born in Barbour Co., June 2nd 1847.
William Alston Ott, son of Edward S. Ott was born in Barbour Co. (Note: Ala.), drowned Chattahoochie River, Ala. June 14, 1866.
Infant of E. S. Ott (Note: no dates given).
Lizzie M. Ott, daughter of E. S. Ott (Note: no dates given).
Edward Dantzler Ott, son of E. S. Ott, born Eufaula, Ala. Sept. 18th 1863, died Oct. 1867.
L. H. Lee, son of Alto V. Lee and Augusta Alston, daughter of A. H. Alston, married in Clayton (Note: Ala.) Oct. 29th 1889.
Augusta Alston, daughter of A. H. Alston, born Eufaula (Ala.) on July 24th 1869, baptized by Dr. Cotten.
A. H. Alston, son of Willis Alston and Anna M. Ott, daughter of E. S. Ott, married Eufaula, Ala., on Dec. 17th 1867.
Edward Ott Alston, son of A. H. Alston, born Barbour Co., (Ala.) March 28th 1871, baptized by Dr. Cotten.
Robert Cotten Alston, son of A. H. Alston, born Barbour Co., (Ala.)
    (Continued)

April 30th 1873, baptized by Dr. Ellison.
J. H. Drake, son of Dr. C. Drake and Lizzie M. Ott, daughter
of E. S. Ott, married in Barbour Co. (Ala. No date given).
Baby boy of A. H. Alston, born in Barbour Co. Nov. 15, 1876, died
Sept. 13th 1876. (This is the correct recording of record).
Anna Louise Alston, daughter of A. H. Alston, was born in Barbour
Co. Aug. 14, 1877, baptized by Dr. Moore.
Philip Henry Alston, son of A. H. Alston, was born in Barbour Co.
Oct. 29th 1880, baptized by Dr. Crawford.
Elizabeth Drake Alston, dau. of A. H. Alston, born in Clayton on
Apr. 17, 1884, baptized by Dr. Crawford.
William Ott Alston, son of A. H. Alston, born in Clayton Jan. 2nd
1887, baptized by Rev. P. P. Winn.
August Houres (?) Alston, Jr., son of A. H. Alston, born Clayton
April 8th, 1890.

HARWELL Bible
Records in the possession of Mrs. S. E. Godfrey, Jr., Eufaula, Ala.
MARRIAGES:
Ishmael Pettway Harwell and Elizabeth Thomas Wade Alston were
married October 2nd, 1813.
Robert R. Harwell & Sally Mason Alston was married the 7th of
December 1809 at Mrs. Martha Hills in Franklin County
North Carolina, Fishing Creek.
Edward J. Harwell and Maria Matheson were married the 7th of
March 1839.
John W. Henley and Evelina T. Harwell were married 18th Feb. 1840
Sarah E. Harwell and John T. Backman See (Lee?) on the
23d July 1846.
Robert R. Harwell Jr. & Mary O. Barnes on the 18th Dec. 1844.
Harriet H. Harwell & Wm. J. Alston 14th July 1847.
Benjamin Glover Shields & Sarah Thomas Harwell were married on
the 26th April 1832.
Ishmael Stirling Harwell and Mary Evelyn Vaughn were married
June 15th 1853.

BIRTHS:
Ishmael P. Harwell, son of Sterling & Mary born May 11, 1789.
Elizabeth Thos Wade Alston daughter of Henry & Sally born in
Warren Co., N. Carolina.
Sally Thomas Harwell first born of Ishl. P. & E. T. W. Harwell
was born Nov. 1st 1814.
Thomas Alston Harwell second born of I. P. & E. T. W. Harwell
was born 25th May 1816.
Ishmael Ganes Dean Harwell the third of I. P. & E. T. W. H. born
October 31st 1817.
A male child not named the fourth born of I. P. & E. T. W. H.
was born on the 9th Jany 1819.
Emmily T. Harwell daughter of Robert E. & Sally was born on 31st
October 1810 Wednesday at Pulleys in Halifax Co., N. C.
Mark W. Harwell son of Robert & Sally was born 24th July 1812 in
Washington County Mississippi Territory.
Harriet H. Harwell was born the 17th Nov. 1814 at Peach Orchard
place.
Evelina Thomas Harwell was born 15th Feby 1817 at Grove Hill now
(Continued).

the residence of Mr. Seth Hunt.
Edward Jones Harwell was born 10th April 1819 - same place.
Robert R. Harwell Junr. was born 4th Jany 1822 - same place.
Sarah Elizabeth Harwell was born 30th Jany 1824 at same place.
Thomas Hill Alston Harwell was born 31st Jany 1827 at Jackson
    Clark County, Alabama.
Sterling Harwell Father of Robert R. Harwell & Ishmael P. Harwell
    was born July 13, 1734 he married Mary Rivers of Virginia
    20th March 1758 & died 15th March 1806. (Note: In the margin
    by this entry is a notation "error to be corrected" that
    has been crossed out).
Ishmael Sterling Harwell son of Robert and Sarah was born
    27th March 1829 at Jackson Clark County, Ala.
A male child still born & the first born of B. G. & S. T. Shields,
    was born on the 18th November 1833.
Harriet Evelina Shields was born on the 24th day of September
    A.D. 1836.
Samuel Robert Shields was born on the 2nd day of November 1827 AD

DEATHS:
Elizabeth Thomas Wade Harwell was delivered of a male child Jany
    9th 1819 which expired in a few hours after she herself
    lingered until the 2nd of February when she died in Jackson.
Ishmael P. Harwell, Jr. had lingered under a consumption for a
    long time   Came from his residence in Jackson to My (?) Robt.
    R. Harwell at Grove Hill and died on a visit to John Mans
    one mile distant 1st April 1820.
Ishmael Ganes Dean Harwell died 11th January 1828 at Tombicbee
    Plantation where he came sick from school.
Robert R. Harwell expired on the 15th of October 1833.
Thomas Alston Harwell died on the 18th Oct. 1834.
Harriet Evelina Shields died on the 10th June 1838 after a long
    and painful illness.
Harriet H. Alston expired on the 10th of October 1848 at her
    mother's in Clark Co. (Ala.).
Sarah Thomas Shields wife of Benjamin G. Shields died on the
    12th of May 1852 at Demopolis, Marengo Co., (Ala.).
Died at 5 o'clock on Sunday afternoon 21st of Feby 1864 at her
    residence in Demopolis Marengo County Alabama Sarah Mason
    Harwell relict of Robert R. Harwell of Clark County Ala. Aged
    75 years and about 2 months.

SPRATLING Bible
Records contributed by Mrs. John W. Curtis, Eufaula, Ala.

Martha Caroline Spratling was born Aug. 29, 1834.
William Philip Spratling was born Oct. 5, 1836.
Benjamin Franklin Spratling was born March 14, 1838, died
    June 17, 1840.
Lindsey Colbert Spratling was born Oct. 15, 1843.
Henry Johnson Spratling was born Feb. 7, 1847.
William Benjamin Barnett was born on Monday the first day of
    Sept. in the year 1851.
Emily Elizabeth Barnett was born Dec. 16, 1812, died
    Nov. 11, 1875, age 62 years 11 months.
Johnson F. Spratling was born May 2, 1857.   (Continued).

Redding A. Spratling was born August 18, 1859.
Nathaniel C. Bridges was born the 23 rd day of January 1818.
Burel J. Bridges was born the 22nd day of Oct. 1819.
Roper C. Spratling was born Oct. 13, 1863, died Dec. 23, 1915.
William James Spratling was born Oct. 7, 1779, died Dec. 1838.
Cynthia Spratling was born April 15, 1783, died Aug. 16, 1828.
Caroline Spratling was born September 12, 1807, died 19th Dec.18
Johnson Spratling was born Sept. 12, 1807, died June 2nd 1849
    age 43.

Betsy E. Spratling was born December 16, 1812.
Cynthia Sara Frances Spratling was born December 27, 1829,
   died Sept. 22 1896.
James Redding Spratling was born December 16, 1831.

DEATHS:
Philip P. Colbert died 23rd of December 1835.
James Spratling died the 16th day of Dec. 1838.
Cynthia Spratling died August 26, 1828, age 45.
Johnson Spratling died 2nd day of June 1849, age 43.

MARRIAGES:
Johnson Spratling and Betsy E. Colbert was married Dec. 19, 1828
Lewis Christian and Sara F. Spratling was married July 20, 1847.
James R. Spratling and M. A. Bailey was Married Mar. 27th 1856.
W. P. Spratling and M. A. Avery was married Oct. 21, 1856.
B. F. Spratling and E. J. Maddox was married 13 Oct. 1859.
William H. Barnett and E. E. Spratling was married Oct. 6, 1850.
Lindsey C. Spratling and Judith Cox was married 2nd March 1865.
Henry S. Spratling and Alamarine David were Married 26 Nov. 1869

WALKER - THOMPSON
(Bullock County, Alabama).

BIRTHS:
Merriott Warren Walker Born March 29th 1834.
Josephine Lancaster Thompson Born Feb. 16th 1841.
Roxana Eliza Goodwin Born Oct. 6th Monday 1845.
Bartow Luther Walker Born Nov. 30th 1860.
Lucy Phillips Walker Born May 16th 1863.
Mary Victoria Walker Born May 28th 1866.
Josephine Irene Bell Born June 14th 1869.
Geo. Henry Walker Born Tues. 5 A.M. Oct. 1st 1871 (or 1876).
William Goodwin Walker Born Sun. 11 A.M. Jan. 21, '77.
Addie Bell Walker Born Tursday 2 P.M. June 28 '80.
Warren Merriott Born Wed. 8:30 P.M. August 30th 1882.
Julia Genevieve Born Tues 3 A.M. Aug. 12 1884.
Annie Walker Born Wed. 4:20 P.M. Sept. 14, 1887.
Warren Warren Walker Born Mon. 5:30 P.M. Sept. 9th 1894. (Note:
   This entry copied as recorded).

MARRIAGES:
M. W. Walker and Josie L. Thompson were married Nov. 1st 1859.
M. W. Walker and R. E. Goodwin were Married Dec. 5th 1870.
B. L. Walker & G. E. Martin were married Jany 25th 1883.
J. E. Parish, Jr. & L. P. Walker were married May 18th 1885.
   (Continued).

G. H. Walker & M. E. McRae were married May 24, 1894.

DEATHS:
Josephine L. Walker died Nov. 1st 1869. (By the side says 1870).
M. W. Walker died Mond. 2:20 July 18th 1887.
M. W. Walker died Wed. 2:30 Oct. 2nd '89. (Note: Duplicate?).

GRIMMETT - HAM Bible
Records in the possession of Mrs. S. E. Godfrey, Jr., Eufaula, Ala.

BIRTHS:
Alfred J. Grimmett Born Dec. 12, 1814.
Elizabeth J. Grimmett Born Oct. 25, 1817.
W. A. Grimmett Nov. 25, 1838.
Mary A. F. Grimmett Dec. 18, 1847.
J. (James) W. Grimmett Oct. 12, 1850.
John S. Grimmett Jan. 6, 1855.
Gideon F. Grimmett Oct. 18, 1858.
Willie F. Grimmett Nov. 27, 1862.
Mary A. J. Goodwin Aug. 17, 1854.
George R. Goodwin Mar. 1, 1856.
J. H. (John Harvey) Ham May 18, 1839.
M. F. Ham Dec. 18, 1847 (Mary A. F. Grimmett above).
W. A. Ham (William Albert) Sept. 6, 1867.
H. J. (Harvey Jackson) Ham June 14, 1873.
Jette Ham Aug. 15, 1875.
Charles H. (Herman) Ham June 28, 1877.
Alfred J. Grimmett Dec. 12, 1815.
Lizzie Verna Ham Dec. 24, 1881.
Winnie Zora Ham Aug. 31, 1887.
Fern Wood Ham Aug. 31, 1891.
Winnie Till Born Mar. 2, 1909 died six hours later.
James Till born Oct. 14, 1910 - died July 18, 1919.
Mary Till born Nov. 1, 1912.

MARRIAGES:
A. J. Grimmett to Elizabeth Tanner Oct. 25, 1837.
Wm. A. Grimmett to Annetta Williams Nov. 25, 1860.
J. H. Ham to M. F. Grimmett Dec. 6, 1866.

DEATHS:
Robert Grimmett died March 1839.
Nancy H. Ramsey July 5, 1850.
James M. Taner Nov. 5, 1850.
Sary Taner Feb. 10, 1842.
Gideon Taner Aug. 22, 1853.
Gideon F. Grimmett Aug. 1860 or 1869 (Note: Hard to read).
W. A. Grimmett Aug. 31, 1862 at Manasses, Va.
John C. Tanner Sept. 14, 1874.
John S. Grimmett Mar. 8, 1876.
A. J. Grimmett June 1, 1881.
Elizabeth J. Grimmett June 7, 1889.
J. H. Ham Aug. 25, 1894.
Willie F. Grimmett July 15, 1865.

GRIMMETT - BROWN Bible
Owned by Ramsey Brown, Tallapoosa County, Alabama.

BIRTHS:
Winston Ramsey Brown born 29 Sept. 1902.
Patsy Ruth Brown born 27 Sept. 1934.
Loucretia Frances Grimmett born 31 Aug. 1860.
George Mike Grimmett born 2 Jan. 1865.
Frances Grimmett born 1865.
Annette Grimmett born 16 Nov. 1870.

DEATHS:
Mary Grimmett died 19 Feb. 1881.
Bob (R. M.) Grimmett died 27 April 1888.
Patsy Grimmett died 8 Dec. 1905.
Wm. A. Grimmett died 8 April 1928.
Frank Lee died 12 July 1932.
Loucretia Frances Lee died 28 Oct. 1943.
George Mike Grimmett died 2 Nov. 1948.
Annette Grimmett Brown died 24 Oct. 1962.

MARRIAGES:
Annetta Grimmett m. Luther Brown 25 Nov. 1900.
Ramsey Weston Brown m. Lallage Gamble 6 Feb. 1926.
Patsy Ruth Brown m. James Walter Hamby 26 July 1956.
Frances Grimmett m. Frank Lee 10 Dec. 1889.
Bill (W. A.) Grimmett m. Ada Murphy Feb. 1899.

SHILOH CEMETERY, Dadeville, Ala.
(Grimmett - Tanner inscriptions only).

Franklin G. Grimmett
18 Oct. 1858 - 2 Aug. 1860

J. S. (Johnnie) Grimmett
Son of A. J. Grimmett
6 Jan. 1851 - 8 March 1877.

Mary E. Grimmett
1848 - 1881

A. J. Grimmett
14 Dec. 1814 - 1 June 1881

Elizabeth Jones (Tanner)
Wife of A. J. Grimmett
25 Oct. 1817 - 7 June 1889

George M. Grimmett
2 June 1865 - 5 Nov. 1948

John C. Tanner
1 Dec. 1829 - 14 Sept. 1874

G. R. Tanner
1826 - 1899

Henry W. Grimmett
Son of J. W. & M. E. Grimmett
15 Dec. 1881 - March 1883

Patsy Grimmett
Wife of R. M. Grimmett
1828 - 1905

R. M. Grimmett
Co. A 47 Ala. Inf. CSA
Died 27 April 1888

Annetta G. Brown
Daughter of Patsy & R. M. Grimmett
16 Nov. 1870 - 24 Oct. 1962

W. A. Grimmett
1855 - 1929

Ada Grimmett
Wife of W. A. Grimmett
1862 - 1901

W. F. Lee
1863 - 1932

Frances Grimmett Lee
Wife of W. F. Lee
1860 - 1948

HAM - FREEMAN Records
Records in the possession of Mrs. S. E. Godfrey, Jr.
Eufaula, Ala.

This is to certify that Milton Samuel Ham and Mary Julia Freeman
were united in Holy Matrimony Dec. 21, 1876 by R. M. Templeton.

BIRTHS:
Milton Samuel Ham Born March 16, 1852
Mary Julia Freeman Born April 5, 1850

Their Children are:
Helen Maude Ham Born Nov. 10, 1877
William Summerfield Ham born Dec. 27, 1878
Milton Clyde Ham born Oct. 13, 1882
Annie Eva Ham born March 5, 1880
Willis Carl Ham born Oct. 3, 1884
Charles Grady Ham born June 16, 1886
Robert Andrew Fisk Ham born May 6, 1889
Charlcie Monterey Ham born Jan. 3, 1892.

MARRIAGES:
Willis R. Ham and Elizabeth Dickey were Married in Elbert Co., Ga.
    Feb. 24, 1834 by Rev. Cantrell.
Dr. J. S. Freeman and M. H. Wiseman were married Dec. 21, 1848 or
    1849 by Rev. Willis D. Mathews.
Willis R. Ham was born Dec. 7, 1809.
Elizabeth A. (nee Dickey) Ham was born Nov. 21 18--
Dr. J. S. Freeman was born Nov. 17, 1827
Mrs. A. Freeman was born July 24, 1833.

HAM Bible
Records in the possession of Mrs. S. E. Godfrey, Jr. Eufaula, Ala.

BIRTHS:
Willis R. Ham was born the 27th of December AD 1809.
Elizabeth A. Dickey now Ham was born 21st of November AD 1809.
Edna Ann Ham was born the 16th of January AD 1835.
Sarah Jane Ham was born the 9th of February AD 1837.
John Harvey Ham was born the 18th of May AD 1839.
William Fletcher Ham was born the 16th of October AD 1841.
Minerva Sophia Ham was born the 29th of April AD 1844.
Susan Elizabeth Ham was born the 23rd of October AD 1846.
Willis Alpheus Ham was born 9th of January AD 1849.
Milton Samuel Ham was born the 16th of March AD 1852.

MARRIAGES:
Willis R. Ham and Elizabeth A. Dickey was married in Elbert County
    Ga. by the Rev. Mr. Crandel February the 24th 1834.
Edna A. Ham daughter of the above named parties was married to
    James B. Sewell by the Rev. W. T. Norman in Elbert County,
    Ga. November the 1st 1855.
Sarah J. Ham was married in Elbert Co., Ga. to C. C. Henry by the
    Rev. G. W. Knight the 27th of April 1857.
John H. Ham was married by the Revt. J. R. Slaughter to Miss Mary
    F. Grimmet in Tallapoosa Co., Ala. on the 6th of Dec. 1866.
Minerva S. Ham was married to James B. Turner by Luke Davenport Esq.
    (Continued)

in Tallapoosa County Ala. on August the 10th 1865.
Susan E. Ham was married to William M. Turner by Revt. D. A.
    Slator in Tallapoosa Co., Ala. on the 15th of Oct. 1871.
Willis A. Ham was married to Mary F. McLendon in Tallapoosa Co.,
    Ala. by B. F. Hammock Esqr. Dec. 10th 1874.
Milton S. Ham was married to Mary J. Freeman by B. M. Templeton
    Esqr. the 21st of Dec. 1876.

DEATHS:
William F. Ham died at Winder Hospital Richmond Va. of wounds
    received in the battle of Spotsylvania on June the 7th 1864.
Willis R. Ham died October 25th 1880.

DANNER Bible
(Barbour County, Ala.)

Purry Locke Danner of Louisville, Ala., m. Annie Gertrude Lott
    of Troy (Ala) on 3 Nov. 1912.
Purry Locke Danner, b. 18 June 1892.
Annie Gertrude Lott b. 27 Dec. 1892.
W. H. Danner b. 15 July 1847.
G. A. Danner b. 12 Nov. 1854.
Arma Leona Danner b. 4 Nov. 1873.
Jullie M. Danner b. 28 Nov. 1874.
T. M. Danner b. 21 Feb. 1877.
W. H. Danner, Jr., b. 8 July 1878.
G. W. Danner b. 4 Feb. 1880.
E. B. Danner b. 15 April 1881.
J. W. Danner b. 2 April 1883.
Mattie M. Danner b. 30 Jan. 1886.
L. M. Danner b. 2 June 1887.
J. N. Danner b. 21 June 1890.
P. L. Danner b. 18 June 1892.
Bessie P. Danner b. 24 Jan. 1896.
Hamner Glen Danner b. Aug. 1913.
Aler Ruth Danner b. 16 April 1915.
Purry Locke Danner, Jr., b. Nov. 16, 1917.
Luther Elmer Danner b. 1 March 1920.
Rubbie Grace Danner b. 22 July 1922.
James Coy Danner b. 17 March 1924.
Annie Bernice Danner b. 24 March 1926.
Era Lorene Danner b. 14 Aug. 1929.
Lena Kate Danner b. 13 Aug. 1932.
Jewel Lois Brock b. 2 Oct. 1932.
Charles Purry Brock b. 24 April 1934.
Cynthia Roberta Brock b. 19 Oct. 1935.
Edward Glen Danner b. 9 Dec. 1935.
Sibil Adreen Danner b. 22 Jan. 1938.
Robbie Virginia Danner b. 3 March 1940.
William Jeter Brock b. 1 Jan. 1938.
Annie Loyd Brock b. 1 March 1940.

DEATHS:
W. H. Danner d. 25 April 1920.
Beulah Ketcham Phillips d. 8 June 1929.
    (Continued).

G. A. Danner d. 30 June 1932.
R. W. Ketcham d. 13 Aug. 1936.
Jewel Dean Danner d. 27 Dec. 1935.
Edward Glen Danner d. 27 Dec. 1935.
Caroline June Danner d.   1935.
J. W. Danner d. 10 Sept. 1939.
Loyd Jeter Brock d. 10 Jan. 1940.
G. W. Danner d. 14 Jan. 1946.
Gladys Danner Blackmon d. 25 July 1946.
Carolyn Danner d. 18 June 1947.
Julia Teal d. 9 Oct. 1947.
T. M. Danner d. 29 April 1948.
E. B. Danner d. 5 Oct. 1948.
Leona Danner Ketcham d. 14 Sept. 1950.
Leon Wilson Phillips d. 24 Sept. 1955.
Bessie Danner Preston d. 5 Dec. 1956.

ABNER WILKERSON Bible

MARRIAGES:
Abner Wilkerson and Miss Matilda Taylor were Married about the
    first of Feb. 1842.
Mr. Abner Wilkerson was Married Second time to Miss Rosaline
    J. Kent Decr. 15" 1863.
Mr. Abner Wilkerson was Married 3" time to Miss Rebecca Parmer
    the first day of Nov. 1881.

BIRTHS:
Abner Wilkerson was born the 16" of May 1818.
Miss Matilda Taylor was born about the first of May 1820.
Miss Rebecca Parmer was born the 8" day of Dec. 1822.
Miss Rosalina J. Kent was born about Jan. 10" 1820.
Frances Wilkerson daughter of A. Wilkerson was born the 9" of
    Feb. 1843.
Lewis Wilkerson was born the 15" Nov. 1844.
Danl Wilkerson was born Oct 23" 1845.
Nora Wilkerson was born 16" of June 1846.
J. P. D. Wilkerson was born Oct. 7" 1850.
Sarah Wilkerson was born June 4" 1853.
Matilda R. Wilkerson was born Sept. 14" 1855
Edmond A. Wilkerson was born Nov. 21" 1857.
Niel J. Wilkerson was born Jan. 24" 1861.
Eunice Wilkerson was Born Oct. 28th, 1884.
Alma Wilkerson was Born March 30th, 1890.
Abner B. Wilkerson was Born Apr. 15th, 1891.
Mary D. Wilkerson was Born May 3th, 1895.

DEATHS:
Mrs. Matilda Wilkerson died about the first of Sept. 1862.
Mrs. Rosaline Wilkerson died June 13" 1881.
Recorded by J. E. Crews June 23" 1882.
Abner Wilkerson Died March 24th 1889.

BENJAMIN SCREWS Bible

J. B. Lippincott & Co., Philadelphia - MDCCCXLIII
    (Continued)

Benjamin Screws & Mourning J. Drake daughter of James and
   Ann Drake of Nash County, North Carolina, were married on
   the 18th day of August on the year of our Lord 1836.
Benjamin Screws was born Decr. 1st 1811.
Mourning Jones Drake was born Nov. 18th 1817.

BIRTHS:
Harriett Ann Screws, daughter of Benjamin & Mourning J. Screws,
   was born in Nash County, North Carolina on the 27th day of
   May 1837.
William Wallace Screws, son of Benjamin & Mourning J. Screws, was
   born in Barbour County, Alabama, on the 25th day of February
   1839.
Mary Eliza Screws, daughter of Benjamin & Mourning J. Screws,
   was born in Barbour County, Alabama, on the 17th of Mar. 184
Benjamin Harrison Screws, son of Benjamin & Mourning J. Screws,
   was born in Glennville, Barbour County, Alabama, on the
   11th day of April 1843.
Caroline Screws, daughter of Benjamin J. Screws & Mourning J.
   Screws, was born in Glennville, Barbour County, Alabama, on
   the 3rd of July 1845.
Henry Preston Screws, son of Benjamin & Mourning J. Screws, was
   born in Glennville, Barbour County, Ala., 10th March 1847.

DEATHS:
Caroline Screws, daughter of Benjamin & Mourning J. Screws,
   departed this life on the 10th day of June 1846, aged
   11 months and 7 days, in Glennville, Ala.
William Wallace Screws died in Coosada, near Montgomery, Aug.
   7th 1913 = buried in Oakwood Cemetery, Montgomery, Ala.,
   died in the 75th year of his life. 1913.
Benjamin Screws died at Shelly Springs, Ala., on the 27th day of
   August 1859. Aged 47 years 8 months & 27 days.
Harriet Ann Garrington died Sept. 5, 1881.
Benjamin Screws died Feb. 22, 1905.
Mourning Jones Drake Screws died 11 p.m. March 4, 1907   aged
   89 years 3 mos. & 14 days. Died in Clayton, Ala.
Henry Preston Screws died at Florala, Ala., 22 July 1918 - age
   70 years & 4 months. Buried in Montgomery Ala.

J. S. WATSON Bible
In the possession of Mrs. J. C. Foley, Eufaula, Ala.

J. S. Watson was married to M. L. (Mary Lenora) McLeod the
   27th Dec. 1877, by Rev. D. C. Crook.
J. S. (James Silvester) Watson was born Oct. 23, 1853.
Mary Lenorah McLeod was born Aug. 10, 1857.

BIRTHS:
Alice Adella Watson was born Sept. 5, 1879, near Batesville,
   Alabama.
James Silvester Watson, (Jr.) was born Feb. 13, 1881.
William Franklin Watson was born Nov. 11, 1886.
Paul Everett Watson was born Nov. 1, 1888.
Walter Lewis Watson was born Sept. 30, 1892.

MARRIAGES:

Alice Adella Watson was married to A. R. Sylvester on
June 10, 1903, by Rev. J. T. Mangum in Birmingham, Ala.
William F. Watson was married to Laura Stuckey Oct. 30, 1911.
James S. Watson, (Jr.) was married to Lillie Crocker June 17, 1912.
Paul Everett Watson was married to Ethel Letitia Yadon on
Nov. 9, 1912, Fort Smith, Ark.
Walter Lewis Watson was married (1st) Willie Taylor, Birmingham,
Ala. Married (2nd) Hazel Kesseler, Birmingham.

DEATHS:
J. S. Watson (Sr.) died Oct. 1895, Batesville, Ala.
James S. Watson, (Jr.) died Mar. 17, 1918, Birmingham, Ala.
Paul Everett Watson died 1940, Kansas City, Mo.
William Franklin Watson died Dec. 1952, Birmingham, Ala.
Ethel L. Yadon Watson died 1953.
Athol Rembert Sylvester died Feb. 14, 1953, Rt. 3, Eufaula, Ala.
Alice Adella W. Sylvester died Sept. 23, 1968, buried Old Spring
Hill, Rt. 3, Eufaula, Ala.

JACKSON - LOCKE - SYLVESTER Bible Records
Bible owned by Mrs. Retta Locke Jackson, Corpus Christi, Tex.

BIRTHS:
Demarcus Sylvester, son of A. (Asbury) and M. (Martha Watkins)
Sylvester, was born in Sumter, South Carolina on the 27th
day of Feb. 1797.
Mary Ann Rembert, daughter of A. (Abijah) and E. (Elizabeth
English) Rembert was born in Sumter, South Carolina on the 29t
of Dec. 1798.
William Herrod Locke, son of Richard and Elvey Locke, was born in
Pike County, Alabama on the 9th of Oct. 1832.
Ann Judson Sylvester, daughter of D. & Mary Sylvester, was born
in Houston County, Georgia on the 1st of Jan. 1838.
Clifford Asbury Locke, son of W. H. & Ann J. Locke, was born in
Eufaula, Alabama on the 1st of Oct. 1860.
Retta Fannin Thornton, daughter of William & Mary Shorter Thornton,
was born in Eufaula, Ala., the 11th of Nov. 1863.
Retta Thornton Locke, daughter of Retta & Clifford Locke, was born
in Eufaula, Ala., on Aug. 20th 1895.
Bush McLaughlin Jackson, son of Mary & James Laval Jackson, was
born in Hagood, South Carolina on Jan. 1st, 1895.
Rhetta Locke Jackson, daughter of Bush M. & Retta Locke Jackson,
was born in Monroe, Louisiana on Dec. 7, 1918.
Bush McLaughlin Jackson, Jr., son of Bush M. & Retta Locke Jackson,
was born in Monroe, Louisiana on Feb. 23rd 1923.

MARRIAGES:
Demarcus Sylvester and Mary Ann Rembert married in Sumter, South
Carolina on the 18th of Feb. 1818.
William Harrod Locke and Ann Judson Sylvester married in Barbour
County, Ala., on the 30th of Oct. 1855.
Clifford Asbury Locke and Retta Fannin Thornton Berry married in
Eufaula, Ala., on the 21st of Feb. 1889.
Retta Thornton Locke and Bush McLaughlin Jackson Married in Eufaula,
Ala., on Aug. 20th 1916.
(Continued).

DEATHS:
Demarcus Sylvester died in Barbour County, Ala., on the 31st of March 1870.
Mary Ann Sylvester died in Eufaula, Alabama on the 22nd of Jan. 1880.
William Harrod Locke died in Eufaula, Ala., on the 15th of Jan. 1882.
Ann Judson Locke died in Eufaula, Ala., on the 17th of Nov. 1912.
Retta Thornton Locke died in Columbus, Georgia on August 4th, 1941. Buried in Eufaula, Ala.
Bush M. Jackson, Sr., died on 27th of April 1954. Buried in Corpus Christi, Texas.

SYLVESTER Family Records
Taken from the LOCKE Bible, owned by Mrs. Mary B. Locke, Birmingham, Alabama, and Sylvester Family History.

Children of Demarcus & Mary Ann (Rembert) Sylvester:
Thomas R. (Rembert) Sylvester was born July 2, 1820, Sumter, S. C.
Mary Ann Sylvester was Born June 29, 1829, in Sumter, S. C.
   Baptised 15 of Oct. AD 1854 by Rev. W. H. McIntosh.
Martha E. Sylvester was born in Sumter, South Carolina on the 26th day of Oct. AD 1831. Baptised on the 14th day of Oct. AD 1853 by Rev. W. H. McIntosh.
Joseph Asbury Sylvester was born in Stewart County, Georgia (Note S. C. in the 1850 Barbour Co., Ala. Census), on July 7th AD 1833.
Ann Judson Sylvester was born in Houston County, Georgia on the 1st of Jan. AD. 1838. Baptised the 13th of Oct. AD Sept. 1852 by the Rev. R. E. Rown.
Fannie (Frances) A. Sylvester was born in Barbour County, Ala., 18th of Nov. 1839. Baptised Sept. 1854 by Rev. William Davis
Camilla Sylvester was born in Barbour Co., Ala., on Sept. 6, 1841 Baptised 18th of April AD 1875 by Rev. William Reeves.

MARRIAGES:
This certifies that Thomas R. Sylvester, son of D. and M. Sylvester and Alethia Beckham, daughter of B. (Burrell) and R. (Rachel) Beckham, were married in Lancaster, South Carolina on the 17th of March AD 1842.
This certifies that Martha E. Sylvester, daughter of D. & M. Sylvester and E. M. Keils were married in Eufaula, Ala., Barbour County, on the 13th of August AD 1847.
This certifies that Joseph Asbury Sylvester, son of D. & Julia F. Woods, daughter of C. and H. Woods, were married in Eufaula, Ala., Barbour Co., on the 25th of Dec. AD 1856.
This certifies that W. H. Locke, son of Richard and Elvey Locke, and Ann Judson Sylvester, daughter of Demarcus and Mary Ann Sylvester, were married in Barbour County, Alabama, on the 30 Day of October 1855.
Colquitt Engram, son of O. and M. Engram, and Camilla Sylvester, daughter of D. & M. Sylvester, were married in Eufaula, Ala. on the 21st of Nov. AD 1864.
Fannie A. Sylvester, daughter of D. & M. Sylvester, and J. M. Thornton were married in Eufaula, Ala., Barbour Co., on (Continued).

the 27th of Jan. AD 1874.

DEATHS:
Demarcus Sylvester died in Barbour County, Ala., on the 31 of March AD 1870. Age 73 years, 1 month and 1 day.
Mary Ann Sylvester died in Eufaula, Ala. on the 22nd of Jan. AD. 1880. Aged 81 years and 23 days.
Joseph Asbury Sylvester died at Richmond, Va. on the 6th of July 1864, aged 31. (Note: Other sources state that he died at Petersburg, Va.) Capt. in CSA. Buried Eufaula, Ala.
William Herrod Locke died in Eufaula, Ala., on the 15th of Jan. 1882. Age 49 years, 3 months and 6 days.
Ann Judson S. Locke died in Eufaula, Ala., on November 17th AD 1912.
Camilla S. Engram died 13 April 1907. Buried in Eufaula.
Frances S. Thornton died 26 Sept. 1927.

Thomas Rembert Sylvester died in Barbour Co., Ala. on Dec. 5th, 1901. Buried at Terese Cemetery, Barbour County.
Mary Ann Sylvester died at Dawson, Ga., on -------- 1928.
Alethia Beckham Sylvester died in Eufaula, Ala. in 1909. Buried at Terese Cemetery, Barbour County, Ala.

PICKETT Bible
Owned by R. B. Guyton, Atlanta, Ga.

BIRTHS:
W. H. Sale, Son of Dudley and Ann Sale, was born March 6 1810.
John H. Harris was born Aug. 3 1778
Frances Rouse wife of W. H. Sale, daughter of John R. and Frances Harris was born October 12 1812 (?)
R. O. Pickett Born June 17, 1863.
Mary Elizabeth Pickett Born April 22 1873
Hiram Steptoe Richard Born Oct. 4 1898
Steptoe Pickett was Born June 21 1816
Eugenia Sale Pickett wife of Steptoe Pickett was born March 26 1834

MARRIAGES:
This Certifies That the Rite of Holy Matrimony was Celebrated Between Richard O. Pickett of Huntsville, Ala. and Mary E. Crumbley of McDonough, Ga. on 26 of December 1897 at Atlanta, Ga., by Rev. C. N. Donaldson of Atlanta Ga. Witness Mrs. Donaldson.
Steptoe Pickett & Eugenia Sale were married the 4th of Sept. 1855.
R. O. Pickett & Mary E. Crumbley were married Dec. 26, 1897.
Hiram Steptoe Pickett and Miss Griffy Guyton July 10th 1919 at Atlanta, Ga., O. B. Landford, Baptist Minister.

DEATHS:
W. H. Sale died August 29 1849
Frances Rousie Sale died Jan 5 1884
Steptoe Pickett, Jr. died August 1882
Eugenia Sale Pickett died 2 March 1907
Richard Orrick Pickett Died May 5th 1929 at Atlanta, Ga.

NATHAN M. BRAY Bible
Published 1854
Bible is in Museum in Eufaula, Alabama

BIRTHS:
Born in Eufaula, Ala. Saturday August 25th 1860 Clifford Wells
    first child of Nathan M. and Catherine E. Bray.
Born in Eufaula Ala. Friday April 25th 1862, Nellie Marks second
    child of Nathan M. and Catherine E. Bray.
Born in Eufaula, Ala. Saturday March 19th, 1864. Kate Ellis, third
    child of Nathan M. and Catherine E. Bray.
Born in Eufaula Ala. Friday Nov. 24th 1865, Joseph Wells,
    fourth child of Nathan M. & Catherine E. Bray.
Born in Eufaula Ala January 18th 1869 Herbert Nathan fifth
    child of Nathan M. and Catherine E. Bray.
Born in Eufaula Alabama Jan 7th 1874 Ethel sixth child of Nathan
    M. and Catherine E. Bray.

MARRIAGES:
Married in Macon Ga. by Rev. Jas. T. Hardenburgh - June 2d
    1859 - Nathan M. Bray to Catherine E. Wells.

Deaths:
Clifford Wells Bray, only child of Nathan M. and Catherine E.
    Bray died in Macon Ga. June 25th 1861 aged 10 months one day
Herbert N., fifth child of Nathan M. and Catherine E. Bray died
    In Eufaula, Ala. March 16th 1870.

PAGE FLOYD Bible
BIRTHS:
Ages of P. Floyd & Elizabeth Floyd parents
Page Floyd was bornd Sept. 26   1816
E. M. Floyd was bornd Oct. the 22   1822

Ages of children:

Henry L. Lange was Bornd the 19   1856
Monro Floyd was bornd Janury = the 22   1859
Nancy Emer Floyd was bornd June 29 in the year of 1864

DEATHS:
Wm. P. Floyd was borned April the 5   1839 and Deceast Jun 5   1863
Louisindy was bornd Oct. 12 in 1840 Deseast Oct. 3   1841
Colin P. was borned May 5   1854 Descesat Jay the 31   1864
Calvin was bornd Oct. 18   1862 Desceast Nov. 19   1863 (?)
Mary C. Floyd was borned Marc the 8   1849 Dide Sep. 28   1849
J. J. Floyd Died July 25th 1881
Elizabeth M. Floyd Died July 2nd 1903.

JOHN BLEDSOE Bible
John Bledsoe and Sarah His Wife were married September 9th 1788.
Keren happuck The daughter of John and Sarah Bledsoe was born
    Novr. 12th and in the year of our Lord 1789.
William the son of John and Sarah Bledsoe was born in the year
    of our Lord March 4th 1791.
    (Continued)

JOHN BLEDSOE Bible continued:
William the son of John and Sarah Bledsoe was born in the
    year of our lord March 4th 1791.
Heathy the Daughter of John and Sarah was born in the Year of our
    Lord October 6th 1792.
Julius the son of John and Sarah Bledsoe was born in the year of
    Our Lord Decr. 22nd, 1793.
Artemisia the daughter of John and Sarah Bledsoe was born in the
    year of our Lord April 19th 1796.
Martha the daughter of John and Sarah Bledsoe was born in the
    year of our Lord Feby. 27 1798
(Name illegible) the daughter of John and Sarah Bledsoe was
    born in the year of our Lord Septr. 2nd 1799.
Emily the daughter of John and Sarah Bledsoe was born in the year
    of our Lord February 28th 1801.
Bud the son of John and Sarah was born in the year of our Lord
    Jany 13th 1803.
Mahala the daughter of John and Sarah Bledsoe was born in the year
    of our Lord Sept. 30 1811(?).
BIRTHS:
Drury Hearn and Keren happcut, his wife was married in the year
    of Lord May 17th 1814.
Abner the son of Drury and Kerenhappuck Hearn was born in the
    year of our Lord Feby 22nd 1815.
John the Son of Drury and Kerenhappuck Hearn was born in the year
    of our Lord Feby 11th 1816.
Sarah the daughter of Drury and Kerenhappuck Hern was born in the
    year of our Lord March 25nd 1817.
Oliver the son of Drury and Kerenhappuck Hern was born in the
    year of our Lord Aug. 22nd. 1818.
Emiline the daughter of Drury and Kerenhappuck Hern was born in
    year of our Lord Decr. 30th 1819.
Edaline the daughter of Drury and Kerenhappuck Hern was born in
    year of our Lord Feby. 4th 1821.
DEATHS:
Tollever The son of Drury and Kerenhappuck Hern was born in the
    year of Lord April 11th 1822.
Jerusha the daughter of Drury Hern and Kerenhappuck Hern was born
    16th July the year of our Lord 1823.
Elizabeth Hern the daughter of Drury and Kerenhappuck Hern his
    wife was born May 26th and in the year of our Lord 1825.
Maryann and Sarahann Hearn was born December 25 1826.
Edmond Hearn was born January 16th 1829.
DEATHS:
Mary Bledsoe the wife of William Bledsoe died Dec. the 8, 1825.
Martha Bledsoe the daughter of John and Sarah Bledsoe died
    July the 26, 1827.
John Bledsoe died November the 24 1829.
Cassandra Bledsoe the daughter of John and Sarah Bledsoe died
    October the 19, 1835.

GOREE Bible
This Bible of Rev. John S. Goree, M. E. Minister at   (Continued).

GOREE Bible continued:
   Robinson Springs, Elmore County, Ala. It was left to his daughter, Mary Elizabeth Goree, who married A. J. B. Rawlinson and is now in the possession of Miss Lydia (Babe) Smith, Eufaula, Ala.

BIRTHS:
John S. Goree was born October 15, 1811.
Nancy Goree was born October 4th 1820.
Mary E. Goree was born February 10th, 1839.
Elizabeth J. Goree was was born August 29, 1841.
John E. Goree was born January 25, 1844.
Harriet C. Goree was born March 15 1846.
Matilda C. Goree was born December 15, 1848.
Mary Smith was born January 25, 1882.
Annie Smith was born August 4th, 1885.
Sallie Mixson Rawlinson was born December 8th, 1861.
Lydia Jane Rawlinson was born August 29th 1868.
Thomas Belle Goree was born November 24, 1867.
Richard Spigener Goree was born Oct. 2, 1870.
Saul Smith was born October 21, 1887.

MARRIAGES:
John S. Goree and Nancy Graves, April 5th 1838.
John Graves, Jr., and Catherine Hogan November 7, 1861.
A. J. B. Rawlinson and Mary E. Goree February 3, 1861.
Mr. John E. Goree and Emma E. Spigener January 10, 1867.
Thomas Light and Hattie Goree 9 January 1868.
John T. Sale and Bettie J. Goree September 2nd 1869.
S. P. Smith and Sallie M. Rawlinson January 20, 1880.
John A. Reese and Liddie J. Rawlinson November 8th 1888.

DEATHS:
Hattie Goree Light died Nov. 6, 1933, Millbrook, Ala.

STROUD - SPEIR Bible
Records are in Eufaula, Ala.

MARRIAGES:
Y. L. Stroud and Sallie Adams was married March 26, 1850.
F. M. Grove and Mary Adams Stroud was married Nov. 14th, 1867.
Wm. H. Speir and Mary Grove was married Nov. 25th, 1873.
David A. Stroud and Lula V. Blalock was married Nov. 2nd 1876.

BIRTHS:
Y. L. Stroud was born 17th June 1829.
Sallie Stroud, his wife, was born 23 March 1834.
Mary Stroud, their daughter, was born 1st March 1851.
David Stroud, their son was born 5th May 1853.
Y. Levi Stroud, their son, was born 20th August 1855.
Theudas Stroud, their son was born 18th Apr. 1858.
Lillias Stroud, their son, was born 28th June 1861.
Homer Speir was born Oct. 18th, 1874.
Lula Speir was born August 13th, 1878.
Lillian Speir was born May 6th, 1884.

DEATHS:
Y. L. Stroud departed this life Aug. 25, 1862. (Continued).

Sallie Stroud departed this life May 20th 1864.
Theudas (Thaddaeus?) Stroud son of Y. L. & Sallie Stroud departed this life May 28th, 1887.
Francis M. Grove died Sept. 21, 1869.
Francis M. Grove, son of Francis M. & Mary Grove, died Oct. 23, 1868.

Stow Bible
Barbour Co., Ala.
Bible owned by Mrs. G. A. Ferrell, Eufaula, Alabama.

MARRIAGES:
Edward Stow and Rabun Susan Brantley, 28 Nov. 1864 at Cotton Hill, Clay County, Georgia.
Lilia Stow and Benjamin Amzi Beach Nov. 9, 1886, Eufaula, Ala.
Rabun Brantley Roberts and George Archer Ferrell 8 Feb. 1918 in Atlanta, Georgia.
Leila Roberts and Francis Collier Rawls 15 April _____ in Prattville, Ala.

BIRTHS:
Edward Stow January 30, 1840.
Rabun Susan Stow September 23 1843.
Rabun Stow September 2, 1865.
Edward Stow, Jr., December 17 1866.
Lelia Stow Jan. 26, 1868.
James Anthony Stow September 7 1869.
Fredonia Stow May 21 1871.
Mary Lizzie Stow October 9 1872.
Addie Stow September 6 1874.
Brantly Stow March 24 1876.
Anthony Stow June 29 1877.
Kate Stow January 6 1879.
Lillie Stow March 6 1882.
Ruth Stow August 21 1883.
Walter Stow February 3, 1885.
Naomi Stow June 23 1888.
George Arch Ferrell, Sr., Sept. 20, 1892.
Oliver Toon Roberts March 1 1869.
Rabun Brantly Roberts May 5 1897.
Mary Roberts (no date).
Oliver Roberts (no date).
George Edward Roberts Oct. 22 1903.
Ralph Roberts Aug. 28 (Year not given).
Leila Roberts Nov. 1 (Year not given).
Adeline Elizabeth Ferrell July 31 1920.
George Archer Ferrell, Jr., April 6 1922.
Toon Roberts Ferrell Nov. 4 1924.
Francis Collier Rawls, Jr., March 22 1936.
Charlotte Raiford Rawls April 14 1938.
Corella Rawls Oct. 8 1941.

DEATHS:
Rabun Stow May 7 1866.
Fredonia Stow March 18 1875.
Lillie Stow September 10 1882.

SOLOMON WALKER Bible
Owned by Mrs. Ed (Dorothy) Morrison, Eufaula, Alabama.
Lewis Walker born North Carolina Jan, 6, 1791. Died Nov. 23, 1877
Nancy McInnis Walker born N. C. Mar. 10, 1810. Died Mar. 29, 1893
Maisy Catherine Walker born Barbour Co., Ala. Dec. 21, 1832.
    Married Arthur Crews. Died Jan. 17, 1889.
Nancy Jane Walker born Barbour Co., Ala. May 16, 1835. Died
    Oct. 23 1929.
Solomon Miles Walker born Barbour Co., Ala. Aug. 14, 1837.
    Died Nov. 10, 1837.
Mary Walker (Thomas) born Barbour Co., Ala. Oct. 6, 1838. Married
    Geo. H. Thomas Feb. 12th 1866, died March 18, 1925.
John Alexander Walker born Barbour County, Ala. Mar. 14, 1841. Di
    a Soldier Civil War Nov. 9, 1862.
Amanda Walker born Barbour Co., Alabama Jan. 1st, 1844, died
    Oct. 13, 1931.
David Lewis Walker born Barbour Co., Alabama Sept. 1st, 1846, die
    March 20, 1935.
James Franklin Walker born Barbour Co., Alabama March 30, 1849,
    died September 25, 1933.
Cynthia Caroline Walker born Barbour Co., Alabama Dec. 19, 1851,
    married Jan. 25, 1870, died Jan 29, 1945.
David A. Wilson (husband) born Barbour Co., Alabama April 12, die
    June 28, 1909.

Grandfather & Mother & Daughter
Solomon Walker *, born N. C. - First from Va. - Aug. 1st 1757,
    died Aug. 11th, 1837.
Gooden (Cox) Walker, born N. C. Nov. 15th 1762, died Nov. 5, 1838
Maisy Walker, born N. C. March 21st 1785, died Aug. 19, 1820,
    buried in Washington Co., Ga.

MOTLEY Bible
This Bible belonged to Rev. John G. Motley. It is now in the
possession of Robert B. Motley, Eufaula, Alabama.

John G. Motley Son of B. K. and Eliz. Motley was born in Autauga,
    Ala., 9th Oct. 1823. Baptized 1840 by Rev. Ebenezer Hearn.
Louisa Motley, Daughter of Shadrick Perry was Born in Muscogee
    Co., Georgia 29 day October 1830. Baptized June 1850 by
    Rev. John W. Talley.
John J. Motley Son of John G. Motley was born in Macon Co., Ala.,
    on 25th Dec. 1849. Baptized June 1850 by Rev. Jno. W. Talley.
John G. Motley Son of B. K. & E. Motley and Louisa Motley, the
    daughter of Shadrick & Eliz. Perry were married in the County
    of Macon 8 February 1849.
John J. Motley Son of J. G. & L. Motley and Eliza O. Hunter were
    married in Tuskegee, Ala., 10 Sept. 1872 by Rev. E. S. Smith.
Robert H. Motley Son of J. G. & L. Motley Born Macon Co., Ala.
    18th October 1851. Baptized by Rev. W. P. Miller. Died Cleve-
    land, Ohio on 19 Dec. 1924.
William Howard Motley Son of J. G. was Born Macon Co., Ala. on th
    20 Dec. 1853. Died Macon Co., Ala. Age 1 year 11 months 20 da

* Not included in Bible Records: Solomon Walker, (Sr.) was a sold
in the Revolution. Buried in Barbour County, Alabama.

MOTLEY Bible continued:
Crawford J. Motley Son of J. G. & L. Motley Born Macon Co.,
   Ala. 27 Feb. 1856. Baptized by C. N. McLeod 21 Aug. 1858
   Died Dallas, Texas 9 Sept. 1891. Aged 35 years, 7 months
   10 days.
Robert H. Motley Son of J. G. & L. Motley and Ellen Graham were
   married in Tuskegee, Ala. (No date).
Crawford J. Motley Son of J. G. & L. Motley, and Tillie Kerr were
   married in Kansas City, Mo., 9 Jan. 1884 by Rev. Jno. Matthews.
Perry Motley Son of J. G. & L. Motley Born in Macon County, Ala.
   on the 1st of May 1858. Baptized August 21, 1858 by Rev. C.
   N. McLeod. Died in Kansas City, Missouri 5th February 1938,
   age 79 years 2 months 24 days.
Perry Motley Son of J. G. & L. Motley and Sallie W. Carpenter
   Daughter of E. W. & M. E. Carpenter, were married in Kansas
   City, Mo. 23 Feb. 1887 by J. O. B. Lowry.
W. W. Thompson Son of W. P. & M. J. Thompson, and Sallie Hill
   Motley Daughter of J. G. & L. P. Motley, were married in
   Pensacola, Fla. on 18 Jan. 1882.
William Magruder Motley Son of J. G. & L. Motley was born in
   Macon Co., Ala. on 10 June 1860.
Sallie Hill Motley Daughter of J. G. & L. Motley was born in
   Macon County, Ala. on 19 Nov. 1862. Baptized 14 June 1863 by
   Rev. F. G. Ferguson, P. E. Named for the wife of Rev. W. M.
   Motley.
Holcombe H. Motley Son of J. G. & L. P. Motley (Incomplete).
Hunter Glenn Motley Son of J. J. & E. H. Motley Born on
   29 June 1873.
John Junius Motley, Jr., Son of J. J. & E. H. Motley born
   15 July 1875.
Hunter Glenn Motley Son of J. J. & E. H. Motley married Eva Lowe.
   (No date).
Howard Crawford Motley Son of J. J. & L. H. Motley Born on
   5 Feb. 1878.
Llewellyn Perry Motley Son of J. J. & L. H. Motley Born on
   1 July 1880. Grandson of J. G. & P. P. Motley
Julia Tignar Motley Daughter of J. J. & E.(?) H. Motley Born
   7 Feb. 1884. Died 6 Sept. 1886.
Howard C. Motley Son of J. J. & E. H. Motley married Gertrude
   Chester. (No date).
Llewellyn Perry Motley Son of J. J. & E. H. Motley married Ella
   Gray Christler(?). (No date).
Edward Cobb Motley Son Of J. J. & E. H. Motley Born Tuskegee,
   Ala. 4 May 1888, grandson of J. G. & L. P. Motley
Nellie Douglas Motley Daughter of E. C. & N. Motley Born Eufaula
   (Ala.) 25 Apr. 1917. Baptized by Rev. Perry Hudson. Great-
   grand daughter of John Glenn & Louisa Perry Motley.
John J. Motley Son of E. C. & N. B. Motley Born Eufaula, (Ala.)
   on 11 Jan. 1920. Baptized by Perry Hudson. Died Eufaula
   20 Aug. 1936. Great grandson of Rev. John Glenn & Louisa
   Perry Motley. Twin of Robert Ballowe Motley.
Edward C. Motley Son of J. J. & E. H. Motley and Nellie Ballowe,
   Daughter of R. A. & N. D. Ballowe were married in Eufaula on
   17 Aug. 1916, by Rev. W. P. Dickinson.
Robert Ballowe Motley Son of E. C. & N. B. Motley Born in Eufaula
   (Ala.) 11 Jan. 1920. Baptized by Rev. Perry Hudson. Great
                                                          (cont).

grandson of Rev. John Glenn & Louisa Perry Motley.
Twin of John J. Motley.
M. Louise Thompson Daughter of W. W. & S. M. Thompson, born in
Tuskegee on 13 April 1885. Baptized by Rev. C. A. Rush. Granddaughter of J. G. & L. P. Motley.
Bessie Thompson Daughter of W. W. & S. M. Thompson, Born in
Tuskegee 25 Oct. 1887. Grand-daughter of J. G. & L. P. Motley.
F. L. Wadsworth Son of F. L. & B. H. Wadsworth married Mary Louise
Thompson, Daughter of W. W. & S. M. Thompson in Tuskegee,
Ala., on 25 Apr 1906.
Bessie Thompson married George W. Griffin in November 1906.
Philip Glenn Thompson Son of W. W. & S. M. Thompson Born in
Tuskegee on 4 July 1890. Married Ethel Henderson, daughter of
J. H. & _____ Henderson at Shorter, Ala.
Watson Crawford Thompson Son of W. W. & S. M. Thompson, born
on 14 April 1893. Died 1893.
Maggie Mae Thompson Daughter of W. W. & S. M. Thompson, born in
Tuskegee 12 Feb. 1895. Died in Tuskegee 9 Apr. 1897. Age 2
years and 2 months.
Gauteir Foster Thompson Son of W. W. & S. M. Thompson Born in
Tuskegee 20 Sept 1897. Married Jane, daughter of J. H. and
_____ Henderson.
Estelle Perry Thompson Daughter of W. W. & S. M. Thompson, born
Birmingham, Ala., 2 Sept. 1901. Baptized by Rev. C. A. Rush.
Married G. W. Turnipseed in Montgomery, Ala. (No date).
Tracy H. Thompson Daughter of W. W. & S. M. Thompson, born in
Tuskegee, Ala., 12 May 1904. Died Sanford, Fla. 2 Dec. 1935.
Married John Paul Belyue (?). (No date).
Robert H. Motley, Jr., Son of R. H. & E. G. Motley, Married
Annie Walker in Union Springs, (Ala.) (No Date).
Jeanette G. Motley Daughter of R. H. & E. G. Motley, Married
A. G. McAndrews in Tuskegee. (No date).
Crawford H. Motley Son of R. H. & E. G. Motley. (No Date).
Graham Motley Son of R. H. & E. G. Motley. Grandson of J. G. &
L. P. Motley. (No date).
Billy Motley Son of R. H. & A. W. Motley. Great Grandson of
J. G. & L. P. Motley. (No date).
Julia Motley Daughter of R. H. & A. W. Motley. Greatgrand
daughter of J. G. & L. P. Motley. (No date).
Ellen Y. McAndrews Daughter of A. G. & J. G. McAndrews, Born in
Tuskegee April 13th 1915. Greatgrand daughter of J. G. &
L. P. Motley.
Jeanette McAndrews Daughter of A. G. & J. G. McAndrews. Greatgrand daughter of J. G. & L. P. Motley. (No date).
Ann McAndrews Daughter of A. G. & J. G. McAndrews. Great-grand
daughter of J. G. & L.P. Motley. (No date).
Hunter C. Motley Son of L. P. & E. C. Motley. Great-grand child
of J. G. & L. P. Motley, Married Inez Windle, daughter of
J. H. & J. Windle. (No date).
Francis L. Wadsworth, Jr. Son of F. L. & L. T. Wadsworth. Born
in Tuskegee May 10, 1907. Baptized by Rev. J. G. Motley.
Died in Tuskegee, Ala. Dec. 13th 1930. Great-grand child of
J. G. & L. P. Motley.
William Thompson Wadsworth Son of F. L. & L. T. Wadsworth. Born
in Tuskegee, Ala., May 9, 1910. Baptised by Rev. C. A. Rush.
(Continued).

Great-grand child of J. G. & L. P. Motley.
Sarah Elizabeth Wadsworth Daughter of F. L. & L. T. Wadsworth, Born in Tuskegee, Ala. on Aug. 22 1912. Baptized by Rev. C. A. Rush. Married Wm. Cooper Smith, Tuskegee on 15th Oct. 1931.
Perry Motley Wadsworth, son of (same parents as above) born in Tuskegee, Ala., 24 June 1914.
Mary Louise Wadsworth (same parents as above) born July 19, 1917.
Ira Virgin Wadsworth Son of (same parents as above) Born in Tuskegee, Ala., 27 Sept. 1922. Baptized by C. A. Rush. Great-grand child of J. G. & L. P. Motley. Grand-child of W. W. & S. M. Thompson.
Rosemary Smith Daughter of W. C. & S. W. Smith. Born in Birmingham, Ala., 26 Jan. 1936. Baptized by Rev. R. L. Bell. Great-grand child of J. G. & L. P. Motley.
Jo Beth Smith Daughter of W. C. & S. W. Smith, Born in Birmingham, Ala., 7 July 1038. Baptized by R. L. Bell. Great-great-grand child of Rev. J. G. & L. O. Motley. Great-grand child of W. W. & S. M. Thompson. Grand child of L. T. Wadsworth.
Jane Gray Motley Daughter of H. C. & I. W. Motley. (No date).
Robert Ballowe Motley Son of Edward & Nellie Motley Born in Eufaula, Ala., 11 day of Jan. 1920. Married Eva Gladys Daniel, Daughter of Mr. & Mrs. J. D. Daniel, in Eufaula, Ala., 2nd Aug. 1947 at the First Presbyterian Church, by C. W. Session.
Carol Elaine Motley Daughter of Robert B. & G. D. Motley born in Eufaula, Ala., on 28th day of May 1950.
Robert David Motley Son of Robert B. & Gladys D. Motley born in Eufaula, Ala., on the 10th March 1953.
Betsy Motley Daughter of Robert B. & Gladys D. Motley born in Eufaula on the 24th day of Oct. 1961.
Nellie Ballowe Motley, daughter of Robert Anderson Ballowe, born in Montgomery, Ala., 1st Oct. 1888. Died in Dathan, Ala., on 22 July 1955. Aged 66 years, 10 months.

GILMORE Bible
Records in the possession of Mrs. S. E. Godfrey, Jr., Eufaula, Ala.
MARRIAGES:
Elijah Gilmore was born the 10th of July AD 1787
Kerren H. Gilmore was born the 23rd of March AD 1793
Elijah Gilmore and Kerren H. Sperlin was Married the 22nd of October AD 1812.
William C. Gilmore was born the 20th of September AD 1813
Nancy G. Gilmore was born the 2nd of April AD 1816
Katharine W. Gilmore was born the 20th of July 1818
Mary Ann Gilmore was born the 31st of December AD 1820
Humphrey S. Gilmore was born the 11th of January 1823
Elijah L. Gilmore was born the 14th of September AD 1824
Stephen G. Gilmore was born the 24th of July AD 1830
Samuel G. Gilmore was born the 17th of October A D 1831

DEATHS:
Stephen G. Gilmore departed this life the 17th of September A D 1831
(Continued).

Elijah S. Gilmore departed this Life 15th of Nov. 1836.
Wm. C. Gilmore departed this Life the 12 of July A D 1854.
Nancy G. Henkle Died the 5th day of June A D 1862 Aged 46 years
    and 2 months.
Samuel G. Gilmore fell in battle near ____ the ____ of May 1864.
George Malcolm Gilmore was born the 10th of May 1834.
Mary Ellen Gilmore was born the 29th of July 1848.
Luther Marvin Gilmore was born the 2nd of Oct. 1867.
Clara Eugenia Gilmore was born the 10th of Nov. 1869.
Nettie Kerren Gilmore was born the 14th of March 1872.
William Early Gilmore was born the 28th(?) of Nov. 1873.
Clara Eugenia daughter of G. M. and M. E. Gilmore departed this
    life Aug. 27th 1871.
George M. Gilmore husband of M. E. Gilmore departed this life
    May 11th 1884.
Mary Ellen Gilmore wife of George M. Gilmore died Sept. 15, 1925.
Nettie Kerren Gilmore daughter of G. M. and M. E. Gilmore died
    August 2nd 1893 (or 1895).

BURCH M. ROBERTS Bible
Owned by Miss Nell C. Holmes, Abbeville, Henry Co., Ala.

Burch M. Roberts married Harriett W. Hardwick Sept. 12th, 1826.
BIRTHS:
Burch M. Roberts bourned in the year of our Lord July 21st 1806.
Harriett W. Roberts borned April 30th 1810.
Children:
Joseph William Roberts borned in the year of our Lord 1827, on
    November 5.
Frances Ann Roberts Bornd Nov. 21, 1829.
Clarisa Jane Roberts borned in the year of our Lord July 25, 1831
Mary Susan Roberts bornd January the 31st in the year of our
    Lord 1833.
George M. T. Roberts borned March 20th 1834.
Richard S. H. Roberts Borned May 10th 1835.
Martha E. H. Roberts Borned Oct. the 25 1839.

DEATHS:
Blurch (Burch) M. Roberts Departed this Life Sept. the 12th in th
    (illegible)year of this age in 1853.
Clarisa Jane Roberts Died September 5th in the year of our
    Lord 1843.
Richard H. Roberts Died Decr. 21st, 1861 aged 26 years, 7 months
    and 11 days.

MARRIAGES & DEATHS:
Patrick B. Skipper & Mary Susan Roberts was married 1847.
Joseph William Roberts & Mary Jane (page torn) was married
    Jan. 18 (page torn).
Micheal Holmes & Martha Roberts was married July 17 1860.
Micheal Holmes departed this life Sept 20th 1886 in the
    59th year of his age.
George W. Holmes departed this life July 22 1906.
Martha E. Holmes departed this life Dec 6 1910.
Alex M. Holmes departed this life Oct. 31, 1912.
    (Continued).

Virginia Holmes Holley died. (No date)
J. Edward Holmes died (No date).

BIRTHS of Micheal Holmes & Martha Holmes:
Virginia E. Holmes was born May 21st 1861.
George H. W. Holmes was born June 4th 1863.
James E. Holmes was born Feb. 8th 1866.
Alex McA. Holmes was born Aug. 11 1868.
Mary A. Holmes was born Dec. 15, 1871.
Hinton C. Holmes was born May 16, 1874.
Annie H. Holmes was born Oct. 22, 1876.
(Page torn) Gillispie Skipper was born Sept. Sept. 26 1850
  Margaret Ellie Skipper was born Apr. 9, 1852.
Birch Skipper was born June 2 1854.
Joseph Roberts Died 22 of October in the year of our Lord 1836.

Children of H. C. & Danie Holmes:
Mike (Micheal) Holmes (born) Nov. 6, 1911.
Mary Helen Holmes (born) Nov. 6, 1911
Nell C. Holmes (born) May 16, 1914.
Gordon W. Holmes (born) Aug. 12, 1916.

TRAMMELL Bible
Owned by Allen Raymond Trammell, Eufaula, Ala.
MARRIAGES:
P. G. Trent M.D. and A. C. Stewart April 23, 1867.
Byron Trammell and Annie Ray Trent Mch 8, 1897
Bryon Trammell Born _____.
Annie Ray Trent Born August 31, 1879.

BIRTHS:
Powatan Green Trent Feb. 13, 1846
America Catherine Stewart Sept 22, 1848
Powatan Green Trent Aug 16 1868.
William Stewart Trent March 26, 1871
Juel Wesley Trent January 22 1874.
Annie Ray Trent August 31 1879 (duplicate).
Morris Whitton Trent Feb 23 1881
Allen Raymond Trammell Mch 14 1898.
Annie Catherine Trammell Jan. 31, 1904.
Stewart Trent Andrews Dec. 7, 1916.

DEATHS:
Morris Whitton Trent Sept. 1, 1882.
America Catherine Trent March 31, 1901.
Powatan Green Trent May 31, 1914.
William Stewart Trent March 24, 1937.
Powhatan Glover Trent March 2, 1922
Juel Wesley Trent Aug. 17, 1944
Annie Ray Trent Brown Dec. 8, 1956.
Stewart Trent Andrews Oct. 31, 1936
Annie Catherine Trammell Apr. 16, 1904.

Memoranda:
P. G. Trent, Jr. Received Baptism Nov. 1, 1873
W. S. Trent Received Baptism Nov. 1, 1873.
(Continued).

J. W. Trent Received Baptism July 6, 1874.
Annie Ray Trent Received Baptism Mar. 10, 1880.
M. W. Trent Received Baptism Mar. 3, 1881.

Children of Allen Raymond & Anabel Dismukes Trammell:
1. Marianne Trammell born 17 Feb. 1932 - married 4 June 1953 to Ross Synder Brown. Their children are:
   Kitty deBrutz Brown, born 27 Apr. 1954.
   Ann Allen Brown, born 21 Sept. 1957.
2. Leita Trammell, born 17 Dec. 1934 - married Elliott Jerry Coleman, Jr., on 24 Aug. 1957. Their children are:
   Elliott Coleman, III, born 8 Sept. 1958.
   Alice Karen Coleman, born 27 Aug. 1963.
3. Allen Raymond Trammell, Jr., born 19 July 1942. Married Joe Ellen McKenney on 9 Dec. 1967.

W. H. CLIATT Bible
Owned by Mrs. Louise Cliatt Martin, Eufaula, Ala.

Presented to W. H. Cliatt by Mrs. W. H. Cliatt, Married May 22, 1885.

William A. Cliatt, wife Elizabeth Blackstock
Children of William & E.
1. William H. Cliatt, wife O'Della Christian
2. Rebecca Albertes (Birdie) Cliatt, husband Alexander Smith

Matthew Averette Died July 1st 1857, age about 70 years.
Daughter Louisa Averette Cliatt, Born May 28, 1824, Died Feb. 26, 1879.

4/30/1839 Fanny A. Cliatt
6/13/1842 William A. Cliatt   7/16/1886
1/13/1849 James W. Cliatt
10/5/1851 Mathew L. Cliatt
1/10/1856 Amie E. Cliatt
3/22/1869 Sarah W. Cliatt

William Henry Cliatt, Born July 11, 1869, Feb. 11, 1932.
Odella Christian Cliatt, Born Feb. 9, 1870, Aug. 10, 1931.

Children of W. H. & Odella
Effie Cliatt, Born March 15, 1898, April 26, 1050.
Tavie Cliatt, Born Dec. 24, 1899, April 27, 1924.
Lewis Albertes Cliatt, Born Oct. 15, 1901, Oct. 1, 1959.
William Leslie Cliatt, Born Sept. 16,
Laura Mae Helton, BornSept. 26, 1916, October 1967.

Willie Cliatt Helton, Born Sept. 27, 1919.
(Mrs. Allen George Heintzelman).

Louise Cliatt, Born March 15, 1924.

Tavie Cliatt Died April 27th 1924.

William Henry, Born July 11, 1869, Died Feb. 11, 1932.
Mable Metcalf Cliatt, Born May 17, 1908, Feb. 12, 1968.

Allen George Heintzelman born Nov. 26 (?) 1918
   husband of Willie C. Helton Sept. 27, 1919.

TAYLOR Bible

Isaac Taylor was Born on the 10 of January in the year of our
    Lord 1780
Isaac Taylor died In the year of our Lord 1829 (or 1849) the
    5th day of February
Dilly Taylor was borned in the year of our lord 1802 October 30
Fanny Taylor was borned in the year of our lord November
    29, 1805.
Nicy Taylor was borned in the year of our lord 1808 - 19th March
William C. Taylor was borned in the year of our lord
    1810 - 28 August
Ardilisa Taylor was borned in the year of our lord 1812
    November 12 day
John W. Taylor was borned in the year of our lord 1815
    14 June
Mary P. Taylor was borned in the year of our lord 1818 -
    July 23
The above Record is the time birth of the children of Isaac
    Taylor & Elender Taylor his wife.
Mary Taylor Lawhon Daughter of Daniel Lawhon & Mary his wife
    was born on the 27 of July 1837.

MARRIAGES:
Daniel Lawhon & Mary P. Taylor was Married the 30th of October
    in the year 1834.

DEATHS:
Dilly Taylor Died the 30 October 1806.
Mary P. Lawhon Departed this life the 6th August in the year
    of our Lord 1837.
Elenor Taylor departed this life Feby 28, 1864 (or 1866)
Pruley(?) Taylor was Borned ye 10 day of November in ye
    year 1777.
Nancy Taylor was Borned ye 20 day January in ye year of 1782.
Samuel Taylor was Borned ye 26 day of January in ye year 1785.
Nicey(?) Taylor was Borned ye 6 day of June in ye year 1787.
Leven Taylor was Borned ye 5 day of July in ye year of 1789.
Thomas Taylor was Borned ye 17 day of March in ye year 1791.
Betsey Taylor was Borned the 17 Day of January in the year 1796.
Saray Taylor was Borned the ___ Day of May in the year 1798.

CHRISTIAN Bible

Lewis Christian was Borne May the 7th 1825.
Cyntha Sarah Frances Spratling was born Dec. 17th 1829.

DEATHS:
Emily E. Christian Daughter of Lewis & Cynthia S. F. Christian
    departed this life December the 4th 1863.
Little Buddy Christian son of L. Christian & S. F. Christian
    departed this life Sept. 22nd 1869.
Alice A. Christian Daughter of Lewis & C. S. F. Christian
    Departed this life Sept. 25th 1869.

MARRIAGES:
    (Continued)

Lewis Christian and Cynthia S. F. Spratling was
  Married July 20th 1847.

BIRTHS:
Emily E. Christian Daughter of Lewis and Cynthia S. F. Christian
  was born July 11, 1848.
Octavia Christian Daughter of Lewis & Cynthia S. F. Christian
  was born August the 7, 1850.
Alice Aliva Christian Daughter of Lewis and Cynthia S. F.
  Christian was born Jan. 28th 1853.
Ridonia Ann Christian Daughter of Lewis and Cynthia S. F.
  Christian was born February 18th 18--.

DEATHS:
(Illegible) Christian, Daughter of Lewis and Cynthia S. F.
  Christian was born Feb. the 28th 1857.
Ila Christian Daughter of Lewis and Cynthia S. F. Christian
  was born May the 15th 1859.
Octavia Christian Died Feb. 3 - 1900.
Ridonia Christian Died Mch. 2 - 1915.
Lewis Christian, Jr. June 17th 1898.
Lewis Christian, Sr., Died Sept 18, 1896.
Frances S. Christian Died Sept. 25, 1896.

BIRTHS:
Lewis Eugenia Son of Lewis and Cynthia S. F. Christian was
  born Oct. the 5th 1861.
Little Buddy Christian Son of Lewis and C. S. F. Christian
  was born Sept. 4th 1863.
Odellar, daughter of Lewis and Cynthia S. F. Christian was
  born Feb. 9th 1866.
Son of Lewis and Cynthia S. F. Christian was born 25 of
  August 18--. (Note: the 1880 Census of Bullock Co., Ala.
  list George Christian, age 10).

MARTIN Bible

Marriages:
John A. Martin and Sarah E. Veal was Married January 13th 1861.
R. R. Martin was Married January 5 1887.

BIRTHS:
John A. Martin was Born January the 6th 1835.
Sarah Elizabeth Martin was Born May the 4th 1834.
Ruben Robert Martin was Born December the 4th 1861.
Sarah Emer Clifford Martin was Born April the 10th 1866.
John Franklin Martin was Born Sept. the 22 1867.
Rufus Agustus Martin was Born Aug. the 3rd 1869.
Carlous Uriah was Born February the 29th 1872.
(Note: rest of page missing).

DEATHS:
John Franklin Martin Departed this life June the 24th 1869 (?).
Sarah J. Veal Departed this life October the fifth 1858.
John T. Veal Departed this life February the 18th 1886.
_____ W. Hall Departed this life January the 19th 1890.
C. M. Roberson Departed this life June 12th 1890.
(Continued).

Loose pages in MARTIN Bible:
BIRTHS:
John T. Veal & Sarah J. Veal was married Feb. the 14, 1833.
John T. Veal was born June the 7th 1810.
Sarah J. Veal was born February the 12th 1817.
Sarah E. Veal was born May the 4th 1834.
William N. Veal was born April the 10th 1836.
Mary Ann Veal was born February the 28th 1838.
Reuben H. Veal was born Dec. the 25th 1839.
James M. Veal was born Oct. the 30th 1841.
Uriah W. Veal was born August the 30th 1843.
Malisa J. Veal was born   the 8th 1845.
Hariet E. Veal was born Dec. the 10th 1847.
_____ E. Veal was born Jan. the 9th 1850.
_____ A. Veal was born Feb. the 8th 1852.

DEATHS:
James M. Veal Departed this Life July the 8th 1862.
Uriah W. Veal Departed this Life May the 5th 1864.
Hariet E. Veal Departed this life July the 22nd 1864.
Reuben H. Veal Departed this life August the 11th 1864.
Mary Ann Veal Departed this Life Sept. the 27th 1874.
William N. Veal Departed this Life June the 16th 1870.
Sarah J. Veal Departed this Life Oct. 5th 1855 (or 1858).

GREEN - OLIVER Bible
Owned by Miss Ethel Blackmon, Eufaula, Ala.
MARRIAGES:
James W. Oliver & Susan Green was married the 1 May 1836, at the
    residence of Mrs. Oliver by the Rev. Mr. King - Mr. J. R.
    Tyson & wife Molie Green Oct. 17, 1865 Tuesday ...At the
    residence of the Brides Father by Rev. Mr. Teat Mr. G. W.
    Oliver & wife Mollie J. Phelps Nov. 16th 1865 Thursday.
BIRTHS:
Susan Green was borned the 21 of January 1808...
Jane Green was bornd the 23 of October 1811...
Francis Green was bornd the 4th of January 1814...
Martha Green was bornd the 18th of February 1817...
Alsy Green was bornd the 31st of December 1825...
Maryann Green was borned the 17th of August 1827...
Julyan Green Decatur was born the 21st of June 1829...
Nelly Green Culpepper was borned the 14th of May 1831...
George W. Oliver was born the 30 of March 1842.
James F. Oliver was bornd the 3rd of May 1852.
Wm. J. Oliver was bornd the 22nd of April 1854.
DEATHS:
George W. Oliver, Sr. dide the 27 March 1836 in the 38 years
    of his age.
Jas. W. Oliver dide May 25th 1857 in the 52nd year of his age.
Jas. F. Oliver died Oct. 28th 1858 in the 6th year of his age.
George W. Oliver died Sept. 15th 1887 in the 45 year of his age.
Wm. J. Oliver died Sept. 17th 1930 in the 79 year of his age.
Verna Oliver died (Incomplete).
Ross Leighton Oliver died (incomplete).
Mrs. Susan Oliver died Oct. 12th 1865 in the 57th year of age.
(Continued).

Frances Green Oliver died March 2nd 1890 in the 76 year
   of her age.
Mrs. G. W. Oliver died (Incomplete).
Joseph F. Oliver died (Incomplete).
Ida Jesse Oliver Powell died (Incomplete)
Mrs. W. J. Oliver died Sept. 24, 1890.
George W. Oliver, Sr. died March 27, 1836 (brother to Jas. W.
   Oliver).
   Entered here by Leila Oliver Watson 1912.
William Jesse Oliver born April 22, 1854.
Wife Mary Lou Taylor born Feb. 22, 1863.
Their children:
James Thaddeus Oliver born Feb. 21, 1879.
Leila Corinne Oliver born Oct. 21, 1880.
Dixie Alma Oliver born Sept. 6, 1883.
Ross Leighton Oliver born Jan. 19, 1888.
Verna Oliver born Sept. 26, 1885.
James Thaddeus Oliver married April 1899, wife Clyde Rogers
   married April 1899, their son
William Thaddeus Oliver born March 25, 1900.
Leila C. Oliver Watson married Dec. 21, 1898 to Huddie
   R. Watson.
Children:
Ross Oliver Watson born Sept. 27, 1900.
George Florry Watson born June 9, 1902.
Wm. Jesse O. Watson born Dec. 31, 1910.
Dixie Alma Oliver married Dec.   to Robert Truitt Watson
Ross Leighton Oliver born Jan. 19, 1888 died Sept. 26, 1900.
Verna Oliver born Sept. 26, 1885, died June 8, 1887.

JOHN BUSHE'S Book of ages

John Bush was born 23d day of December in the year of our
   Lord 1787.
John Bush was married to Frances Johnson the daughter of Hugh
   Johnson & Frances 27th October in the year of 1814.
Frances Bush wife of John Bush was born the 9th day of
   August in the year of our Lord 1801.
Eliza Bush was born the 20th day of February in the year of
   our Lord 1817.
Cynthia Bush was born the 20th day of Nov. in the year of our
   Lord 1818.
Harriet Bush was born the 17 day of October in the year of
   our Lord 1820.
Isaac Bush was born the 6th day of November in the year of
   our Lord 1822.
William Prescott Bush was born the 12th day of December in
   the year of our Lord 1824.
My Son John Bush was Born January the 12th 1827.
Richard H. Bush was Bornd the 19th day February 1829.
Elcy Ann was born in the year 1831 and on 20th Day of May.
Frances Bush was Borne the 17 October 1833.
Silas Bush was born the 19th day of November 1835.
Matthew Boosh (Bush?) was Born on the 17 of december 1837
Susanna Bush daughter of Frances & John Bush was born Feby
   3d, 1840. (Continued).

Mary Ann Bush was born April 3rd 1842.
Anney D. Bush was born May 6" 1844.
Marcus D Lafayett Bush was born Apriell the 11   1848.
T. J. L. Phillips was borned March the 3 1838
Anna Dhillips (Phillips?) was bornd May the 6 1844.
Joseph Wm. Phillips was borned December the 19 1859.
John R. Phillips was borned March the 19 1862
James M. Phillips was bornd August the 10 in the year of
    our lord 1866.

ANDREWS Bible
Records owned by Mrs. S. E. Godfrey, Eufaula, Ala.

BIRTHS:
Ann Andrews born at Wascan (Waxhaws?) S. C. June 1780.
Mary Burr Andrews born at Newport October 25 1786.
Matilda Hull Andrew(s) born Washington (Ga.?) 21 Sept. 1792.
James Osgood Andrews born D   May 3rd 1794.
Charles Godfrey Andrew(s) born Long Creek July 10th 1795.
Lucy Garland Andrew(s) born Elbert (Co., Ga.?) Aug 25, 1799.
Betsy Sidnor Andrew Born Elbert (Co., Ga.?) October 28, 1800.
Cynthia Fletcher Andrew born May 1st 1802 Elbert Co.
Caroline Wesley Andrew born 13 Aug. 1804.
Lucy Evilina Andrew born 27 Dec. 1805 Elbert Co.
Henry Andrew born 7th Dec. 1809.
Hardy Herbert Andrew born Elbert Co. 17 March 1811.
William Harvie Andrew born 18th Sept. 1813 Elbert Co.
Two children, not named, who died monents after birth.
Elizabeth Mason Andrew born Wilmington, N. C. April 4, 1817.
    daughter of James and Amelia Andrew.
Mary Overton Andrew born (date blank), daughter of James and
    Amelia Andrew.
Frances Mildred Spencer born April 7th 1814 Elbert Co.
Mary Overton Spencer born Elbert Co. 11 Sept. 1814.
James Andrew Spencer born Oglethorpe Co. Dec. 3, 1816.
Overton Fletcher Davenport born Oglethorpe Co. 1/10/1820,
    son of William Davenport and Betsy.
Lucy Davenport (no dates, may be mother of John Andrew Wright).
John Andrew Wright, son of John and Lucy Wright.

DEATHS:
Charles Godfrey Andrew died 5 Oct. 1796.
Scynthia Fletcher Andrew Dec. 5, 1803.
John Andrew died in Clark Co. Mar. 10, 1830, age 72½ years.
Judy Harvey Andrew (daughter of John and Mary O. Andrew) died
    Clark Co. June 23, 1833.

MARRIAGES:
John Andrew was married to Ann Lambright 10 Feb. 1779 at the
    Evharms (?) South Carolina by Rev. Goneerly.
John Andrew m. Mary Burr Andrew 20 Sept. 1785 Colo (?) Island.
John Andrew m. Mary Overton Cosby in Elbert Co., Ga. 11 Dec. 1795.
James O. Andrew m. Ann Amelia McFarlane on 1 May 1816 in
    Charleston, S. C.
Betsy Sidner Andrew m. William Davenport 10 Dec. 1811 (?).
(Continued).

Ann Andrew (dau. of John and Ann) m. Abram I. Roberts
at Coon Sahatchie (no date).
Lucy G. Wright m. Wm. R. (illegible, may be Nesing) Nov. 30,
1844.
Mary Burr Andrew (dau. of John and Mary) m. Samuel Lesueur at
Elbert Co., Ga. 2 July 1807.
Matild Hull Andrew (dau. of John & Mary O.) m. George G. Spencer
on 14 Dec. 1809 in Elbert Co., Ga.
Lucy G. Andrew m. John Wright in Clark Co., May 10, 1830.

Notes on births:
Ann, daughter of John and Ann Andrew, was born at Wascan (?)
S. C. on 20 Jan. 1780.
Mary Burr, daughter of John and Mary Burr Andrew, was born
Newport, Ga. on 26 Oct. 1786.
James Osgood Andrew, son of John and Mary O. Andrew, born
8 May 1796 in Wilks Co., Ga.
Matilda Hull Andrew born Wilks Co., 25 Sept. 1792.
Charles Godfrey Andrew born Oglethorpe Co. on 10 July 1795.
Lucy Garland Andrew born Elbert Co. 26 Aug. 1799.
Betsy Sidnor (or Sidner), Elbert Co., 28 Oct. 1800.
Scynthia Fletcher Andrew born 1 May 1808 Elbert Co. (Note: one
child by this name born 5 Dec. 1803).
Caroline Wesly Andrew born Elbert Co. 13 Aug. 1804.
Patsy Evelina Andrew born 27 Dec. 1806 Elbert Co.
Judy Andrew Harvey born Elbert Co. 7 Feb. 1809.

Additional notes on face of New Testament section:
William Harvie Andrew born 19 Sept. (date torn) - another child
was baptized by the same man in 1813.
---indy Herbert Andrew born 17 March 1811.

MCKENZIE Bible
Records obtained from Mrs. John Curtis, Eufaula, Ala.

William McKenzie born April 25th, 1805.
William McKenzie died Nov. 18, 1846.
William McKenzie married July 19th, 1824.
His wife Susan born Dec. 5, 1805.
His wife Susan died Nov. 22, 1863.

Children:
James William McKenzie born April 16, 1827.
Laura Ann McKenzie born Dec. 4, 1829
Laura Ann Horne died Jan. 14, 1870.
John Henry McKenzie born March 2, 1832.
Malissa Evaline McKenzie born Oct. 19, 1834.
Malissa Evaline Walters died Feb. 17, 1865.
Alonzo Sutton McKenzie born Jan. 16, 1837.
Roxana Victoria McKenzie born June 28, 1839.
Martha Ann Josephine McKenzie born Nov. 26, 1843.
Martha Ann Josephine Westbrook died July 30, 1873.

Family of:
James William McKenzie born April 16, 1827.
James William McKenzie died April 15, 1907.
and
Lavinia Burnam born Nov. 1, 1835.   (Continued)

Lavinia Burnam married April 10, 1851.
Lavinia Burnam died Dec. 12th 1901.

Children:
Susan Cecilia McKenzie born March 17, 1852.
Susan Cecilia McKenzie died July 24, 1852.
John William McKenzie born July 12, 1853.
John William McKenzie died Oct. 7, 1853.
Lounella Lorette McKenzie born Nov. 4, 1854.
Lounella Lorette McKenzie died Sept. ___ 1903.
Lounella Lorette McKenzie married Edd Westbrook.
Laura Ann McKenzie born April 15, 1857, married Middleton
    McDonald, who died and then she married Jim Pate.
Lizzie Ada McKenzie born Feb. 12, 1860, married Bob Davis
Milissa Lenore McKenzie born May 15, 1862, married Eugene
    Turner who died and then she married L. F. Coxe.
Martha Ann Josephine McKenzie born Oct. 3, 1866, married
    Bob Sutton.
Irene McKenzie born March 22, 1868.
Irene McKenzie died Oct. 10, 1879.
Willie Elma McKenzie born May 30, 1871, married A. T. McKenzie.
James Alonzo McKenzie born Dec. 18, 1877.
James Alonzo McKenzie died Feb. 2, 1902.
Lionel Wilfred McKenzie born April 9, 1880.

BOWERS Bible
Bible written in German - was found in an antique shop in
Damacus, Early County, Georgia.

Trauungen:
Martin Bowers and Fanna Berg were married March 8th AD 1838
Martin Bowers and Jane Keefer were married December the
    10th AD 1846.
Martin Bowers was born April 3 AD 1817
Fanna Bowers was born June the 16th 1818
1. Benjamin Bowers was born february 28th 1839
2. Anna Bowers was born August 19 AD 1840
3. Abraham Bowers was born October 18th AD 1841
4. Elizabeth Bowers was born December 15th AD 1842
5. Lusana J. Bowers was born December 11th AD 1847
6. Mary D. Bowers was born July 3 AD 1850
7. Joseph Bowers was born April the 26 AD 1854
8. Moses Bowers was born December the 8th AD 1856

Gterbefalle:
1840 Nov. 20th Anna Bowers dept. this life age 3 mo & 1 da.
1841 May 3 Benj. Bowers departed this life age 2 yrs 2 mo 3 das
Mother
1844 Mar. 9th Fanna Bowers departed this life age 26 yrs. 4 mo
    24 days.
1855 Sept. 29th Joseph Bowers departed this life
    age one year 5 months 2 days.
1861 March 17 Elizabeth Bowers departed this life
    age 24 years 3 months 2 days
Abraham Bowers died July 29, 1885 age 45 years 9 months 10 days
(Continued).

Moses K. Bowers died at Harrisburg, May 1, 1897,
   age 40 years 4 months 23 days.
1893 June 24 Father Martin H. Bowers, Mechanicsburg, Pa.
   Sat. morning June 24, 1893, age 76 years 2 months 21 days.
Mother, Christena Bowers died June 28 1907 age 89 years and
   7 days at Mechanicsburg, Pa.

THOMAS Bible
Owned by Mrs O. D. Hooper, Eufaula, Ala.
CERTIFICATE:
This Certifies that the rite of Holy Matrimony was celebrated
   between John Curtis Thomas of Eufaula, Ala. and Miss Mattie
   Virginia Allday of Eufaula, Ala. on the ninth of June 1863
   at the home of the bride's mother, by Joseph Benson Cottrell
   of the Ala Conf. of the M. E. Church, South.
BIRTHS:
Mattie Crocker Thomas Friday June 23, 1865 1:30 P.M.
Annie Virginia Thomas Tuesday Nov. 12, 1867 5 A.M.
Edith Curtis Thomas Wednesday March 15, 1871 5:30 P.M.
John Cortez Thomas Tuesday March 3, 1874 1 P.M.
Arthur Morse Thomas Sunday June 3, 1877 12:52 A.M.
Nelly Thomas Saturday Feby 22, 1879 3:15 A.M.
Herbert Spencer Thomas Friday Nov. 17, 1882 12:15 P.M.
Agatha Tully Wednesday Sept. 8, 1886 9 P.M.
Annie Thomas Tully Friday Dec. 9, 1887 2 P.M.
Randolph Rusk Thomas Friday April 12th 1889 10 P.M.
Kathleen Curtis Tully Sunday Sept. 1st, 1889 4:50 A.M.
Daniel Thomas Tully Thursday Sept. 15th, 1892 2:10 P.M.
William Mallory Tully Thurs. Mch 10th 98 2:18 A.M.
Olivia Thomas Tully Tuesday April 14 1903 9:05 A.M. in
   Buffalo, N. Y.
John Cortez Thomas, Jr., Wednesday Mch. 29th 1905 4:30 P.M.
   (illegible), Ala.
Edmund Mooney Tully July 30th 1906.
Randolph Hinton Thomas Sunday Feb. 16, 1913 11:15 A.M.
   Woodbury, Ga.
John Curtis Thomas II Wednesday Feb. 11, 1914 at Woodbury, Ga.
Mary Virginia Thomas Monday June 1915, Woodbury, Ga.
Kathleen Virginia Garvin, Tuesday November 5th 1929 - 12 A.M.
   Jefferson Barracks, Mo.
Geo. Thomas Garvin born Dec. 21, 1934 Ft. McPherson.
Daniel Tully Garvin, Sunday Mch 9th 1924 Fort Benning, Ga.
Ford Morris Garvin, Monday Jan. 11th 1926 - 5 P.M. Manilla,
   Phillipine Islands.
Julian J. Thomas & William J. Thomas, Monday Oct. 20th 1919,
   Woodbury, Ga.

MARRIAGES:
John Curtis Thomas - Mattie Virginia Allday, Tuesday June
   9, 1863, 8:30 P.M.
William Marcellious Tully - Annie Virginia Thomas - Wednesday
   April 22nd, 1885 3:30 P.M. Rev. R. Fullerton.
Charles Mallory Thompson - Mattie Crocker Thomas Wednesday
   Dec. 17th, 1902 - 6:30 P. M. - Rev. H. B. Wharton assisted
   (Continued)

by Rev. J. A. Peterson.
John Cortez Thomas - Eleanor Egletine Boylston - Thursday Dec. 25th 1902, 6 P.M., Rev. J. U. Graf at Apalachicola, Fla.
Randolph Rusk Thomas - Willie Mae Hinton, Wednesday May 1st, 1912 - 7 P.M. - Rev. J. D. Carriker - Malena, Ga.
Edmund M. Tully - Bettie Wandland, New York (Note: no date given- ca 1933).
Mary Virginia Thomas - James Edwin Wells, June 8th 1940 - Rev. Woosley E. Couch, College (illegible).
James Thomas Wells, Oct. 23, 1941, Bermuda Island (Note: this is a birth).
George Crump Garvin, Lieut. USA - Ollie Thomas Tully, Tuesday Sept. 26th 1922, Church of the Holy Family, Columbus, Ga. Rev. Joseph Marlon, Rev. J. McCormick, Rev. Lehan, USA.
Ono David Hooper - Kathleen Curtis Tully, Monday, Mar. 28th, 1910 10 A.M. - Rev. J. Sweeny - Church of the Holy Redeemer, Eufaula, Ala.
Randolph Hinton Thomas (illegible) Jan. 25, 1926.
Mary Joyce Thomas, Nov. 1939. (Note: this is a birth).

DEATHS:
Edith Curtis Thomas, Sunday, June 2nd 1872.
Arthur Moore Thomas Monday Decr. 31, 1878.
Nelly Thomas Monday June 30, 1879.
Agatha Tully Wednesday Sept. 8th, 1886 10:31 P.M.
Annie Thomas Tully, Sunday Dec. 21st, 1890 2:30 P.M.
John Curtis Thomas Tuesday Aug. 18th 1891 2:15 A.M. "Our Papa"
William Mallory Tully Tuesday June 28th 1904 6 P.M. at Buffalo
John Cortez Thomas, Jr. Wed. Apr. 19th P.M. at Montross, Ala.
Eleanor Egletine Boylston Thomas Thursday April 20th 1917 10: 25 P.M. at Montross
John Curtis Thomas II Feb. 11 - 12 o"clock
Mattie Virginia Allday Thomas Sunday Oct. 28th 11:05 P.M. "Our Mama". (Note: year not given, but Mrs. Hooper says 1918).
Daniel Thomas Tully Sept. 4th 1919 - Tours France near Paris in U. S. Service 35th Service Signal Corps. Sargt. Maj. (Note: Mrs. Hooper says he is buried at Arlington Cemetery).
William Marcellus Tully Jan. 17th 1917, Buffalo, N. Y.
Charles Mallory Thompson, July 9th, 1933, Sunday 9:25 P.M.
John Cortez Thomas, Tuesday May 8th 1934 1:30 A.M.
Ono David Hooper, Sept. 14, 1936 - 1:10 A.M.
Randolph Rusk Thomas, Aug. 18, 1941 - 12:15.
Annie Thomas Tully, Dec. 4th   5 P.M. Eufaula (Alabama).
Mattie Crocker Thomas Thompson, 11 Feb. 1948, Eufaula. Ala.
Herbert Spencer Thomas, 17 April 1966, Eufaula, Ala.

SPURLIN Bible
Records furnished by Mrs. Sam Godfrey, Eufaula, Alabama

James Spurlin Sone of Wm. Spurlin was borned the 20th of June AD 1802.
Nancy Michel but know (now?) Spurlin daughter of Starling Michel was borned the 18th of August AD 1808.
William Spurlin son of John Spurlin and Myally his mother was borned the 12 of January AD 1769.
    (Continued).

DEATHS:
William Spurlin son of John Spurlin and Myally his mother
  departed this life the 30th of April AD 1835.
Nancy Spurlin departed this life December 13th 1875.
William G. Spurlin departed this life a prisoner of war at Fort
  Delaware, U. S., on July 15th 1864.
James A. Spurlin was killed at Battle at Malvern Hill, Va. on
  July 1st, 1862.
Amanda S. Spurlin departed this life August 23rd, 1863.
Columbus G. Coggin died in the Virginia army June 25, 1862.
James S. Coggin, son of C. G. & Frances M. Coggin departed this
  life the 18th of November AD 1861.
James Spurlin departed this life the 18th Nov. AD 1887.(Son of Wm

MARRIAGES:
James Spurlin Booke bought of Wm. Whit in Pike County (Ga.) and
  505 Dist. G. M. On the 4th of July A.D. 1836 and the Sisethe
  yer of Independency of the U.S.A. Price, 5, 18.
James Spurlin and Nancy his wife was married on the 10th of
  December AD 1829.
Columbus G. Coggins and Frances M. Spurlin were married
  December 24th 1854.
William J. Newell and Frances M. Coggin were married
  Feb. 15th 1866.
William G. Spurlin and Lydia Coats were married December
  29th 1859.
Joseph M. Scott and Rhoda O. Spurlin were married Jan. 28th 1866.

Children of Joseph M. Scott and Rhoda Spurlin Scott:
  Ida Inez Scott - Wept. 12, 1868.
  Zachary Lumpkin Scott - Sept. 26, 1871.
  Jessie James Scott -- June 23, 1876.

  Lucy Kate Scott -- June 6, 1879.
  Eugene Fred Scott -- Feb. 4, 1889.

BIRTHS:
Frances M. Spurlin daughter of James Spurlin and Nancy her mother
  was borned the ____ day of March AD 1831.
Wilson L. Spurlin son of James Spurlin and Nancy his mother was
  bourned the 14th of May AD 1832.
Wm. G. Spurlin son of James Spurlin and Nancy his mother was
  borned the 28th of January AD 1836.

DEATHS:
Cloudy H. Spurlin daughter of William G. Spurlin and Lydia her
  mother departed this life October 25, 1863.
William Charles Spurlin son of William Spurlin and Liddie his
  mother departed this life Sept. the 17th AD 1887.
Sarah Spurlin, wife of William Spurlin, departed this life in
  her 90 secon year November 4 AD 1859.
Martha Ann Spurlin daughter of James Spurlin and Nancy her mother
  departed this life July 22 AD 1894.

BIRTHS:
James A. Spurlin son of James Spurlin and Nancy his mother was
  borned the 8 of September AD 1838.
Amanda Samarines Spurlin daughter of James Spurlin and Nancy her
mother was bornd the 28 of Jan. AD. 1841.   (Continued).

James Silas Coggin son of C. G. and Frances M. Coggin
   was born Nov. 25th 1855.
Daniel W. Coggin was born Sept. 29th 1857.
Virginia Davis Coggin was born July 2nd 1860.
Wm. Charles Spurlin son of Wm. G. and Lydia Spurlin was born
   Feb. 1st 1864.
Lydia Spurlin was borned Feb. 29 AD 1835.
Martha An E. C. Spurlin daughter of James Spurlin and Nancy her
   mother was bornd 28 of December AD 1843.
Rhoda Obedience Spurlin daughter of James Spurlin and Nancy her
   mother was bornd the 2 of July AD 1846.
Cloudy W. Spurlin was born the 7th of November 1860.
Sarah F. Newell was borned June the 20 AD 1867.
Nancy D. Newell was borned March the 25 AD 1869.

(Note: On a separate page, but enclosed in Bible).

Robert Scott born 1809.
Mary Scott born Jan. 8 1812. Died Mar. 16, 1863.
Robert Scott died Oct. 21, 1847.
Children of Zachery Lumpkin Scott and Sallie Lou DuPree Scott:
Ruth (Mrs. Roy C. Sasser).
Irene (Mrs. E. L. Sasser).
Alma (Mrs. A. J.   )
Annie Kate (Mrs. D. P.   , Jr)
Theo (Mrs. A. A. Grenee) July 2, 1901
Corinne (Mrs. John H. Hartley) July 25, 1905.

ROBERT CARAWAY Bible

BIRTHS:
John M. Caraway was bornd April the 22, 1820
Archabel E. Caraway was born March 31th, 1822
Mary E. Caraway was born November 5th 1824
Jane Caraway was born July 31th 1826.
Ann Caraway was born July 1th 1828
Lucy C. Caraway was born March 27th 1830
Verlinda C. Caraway was born April the 27 1832
George W. Caraway was born April the 8 1838
James A. Caraway was born December 27th 1839
Sarah E. Caraway was born August 27th 1841
Demais (?) A. Caraway was born January 11th 1844
Emily P. (?) Caraway was born Febuary the 1 1846
Robert S. Caraway was born April the 21 1849
Josephine C. Caraway was born September the 16 1851.
William L. E. Caraway was (born) febuary the 10 1854
(Note: Robert Caraway m. first Mildred McCorkle, second Augusta
   Ann Green).

DEATHS:
Mildred Caraway the wife of Robert Caraway Departed this life
   April the 6 1834
Jane Caraway the Daughter of Robert Caraway Departed this life
   September 1827 (or 1829)
      (Continued).

Robert Caraway Departed this life May the 20   1856.
Josephine C. Caraway Departed this life June 6 1859 (?).
William L. E. Caraway Departed this life June the 17   185-.
George W. Caraway Departed this life October the 17   1861
Lucy C. Caraway Departed this life October the 10th 1863. (?)
Archibel E. Caraway Departed this life August the 3 1864.
William F. Caraway Departed this life Febuary the 8 (or 28) 1870
Irene Brown departed this life december 31   1898, Age 42 years.

BIRTHS:
Arrina Caraway was born July 14   1856
Augusta Ann Caraway was born January the 1 day 1822
Thomas E. Caraway was born March 15   1868
William F. Caraway was born January the 2   1870
C. M. Caraway was born Feb. the 9 1857 (?)
L. L. Brown was born September the 12 1857
Franklin Julius Brown was born March the 11   1885
Mary   Brown was Born October the   1887
Austin Brown was born Sept the 17th 1890
Effy Irene Brown was born October the 8th 1892
H   Brown was born August the 1st 1894 (?)

MARRIAGES:
Robert S.(?) Caraway and   M. Fincher was married Dec. the
    8 (?) 1878 (?).
L. L. Brown and   Caraway was married Januy the 6th   1884
L. L. Brown and Mattie Durham was married feb. 1899
Franklin J. Brown and Mary Etta Durham was married Jan. 31, 1904.

NATHAN SIMPSON TEW Bible

MARRIAGES:
N. S. Tew and Emma Caraway was married December 30, 1900
N. S. Tew and Annie Parmer was married August 3, 1913
Edward N. Tew and Elizabeth Lanier was married July 1925
Comer L. Tew and Corinne Johnson was married August 4, 1928
Marvin C. Tew and Neely Thomley was married October 1928
Lucille Tew and Ike (?) Stuckey were married Sept.   1933.
Myrtle Tew and Grady Folkes were married Oct. 28, 1933
Dixie Tew and Lee (?) Davis (?) were married Nov. 1, 1933

BIRTHS:
Hezekiah Tew was born Sep. 6th 1836
Sint Tilly Tew was born June 5th 1844
Henry Caraway was born Nov. 24th 1853
Mandia C. was Born Nov. 9 1851
N. S. Tew was born May the 12th, 1881
Emma Tew was born Sept 16th, 1881
Edward N. Tew was born September 20th, 1903
Comer L. Tew was born November 20, 1905
Shelley Tew was born May 23rd, 1907
Marvin C. Tew was born Nov. 28th 1908
Mamie L. Tew was born June 30th, 1911
Sary Annie was Born Oct. the 8, ----(?).
Alcy M. Tew was Born _____(?).
Dixie M. Tew was Born Sept. 9th, 1916.
Nathan W. Tew was Born May 17th (?), 1919.
(Continued).

(Illegible) C. Tew was Born ----------- 1921.

DEATHS:
First son died March the 29th, 1902, the Second son died September the 20th, 1903.
Emma Tew died March 23, 1913
N. S. Tew died March 16th, 1925
Henry Caraway Died Apr. 26 1892
Mandia C. Died Sept. 8, 1912.

(Note: Parts of this Bible were illegible).

ANDRESS Bible

Records contributed by Mrs. John W. Curtis, Eufaula, Ala.
Stephen S. Andress was born 13 December 1797. *
Susan McCoy was born April 5, 1797. *
Francis M. Andress was born Sept. 23, 1820.
Redden McCoy was born 20 Oct. 1822 South Carolina.
Mary Jane Andress was born Oct. 30, 1822.
Susan Carolina Andress was born 2nd day of Oct. 1824.
Stephen Decatur Andress was born Aug. 12, 1827.
Hamton Monroe Andress was born 29 Oct. 1829.
Nancy Andress was born 22nd of August 1832.
Mary Sallie was born 25 Oct. 1839.
George Harmer was born 22nd Dec. 1840
Frances was born 30 August 1842.
Nelson was born 8 Aug. 1841.

DEATHS:
Nancy Andress Deceased on the 4th day of August in the year of Our Lord 1840.
S. S. Andress departed this life 13 Nov. 1861.
Mary Jane Davison departed this life on 19 Jan. 1862.
Joseph N. Andress departed this life on the 23rd of May 1861 - Pensacola, Fla.
W. T. Andress departed this life 21 day of July 1863 - Gettysburg.
Redden M. Andress was killed the 21 of July 1863 - Battle before Atlanta, Ga.
Susan Andress departed this life on the 12th day of April 1882.
Francis Marion departed this life March 23, 1888.
Decatur Andress & Martha Nettles was married 10 Feb. 1848.

JOSEPH ANDRESS Bible
Xerox copy of the original in the possession of Mrs. John W. Curtis, Eufaula, Ala.

Joseph Andress was borned on the 8th day of August 1734.
William Andress was borned the 22nd of October 1736.
The above named Brothers Joseph & Stephen came to America from (Continued).

Redden McCoy came from Scotland and married Susan Jane Pringle, S.C. and moved to Ala. Their child Susan Jane McCoy married Stephen Singleton Andress 12/23/1819.

England in the year of 1754.
William came South and the ancestor of our immediate family.
  He Settled in Robeson county North Carolina. Joseph
  (illegible)........no Record......destiny........
William was borned September the 8th 1778, S. C.
Ann Rhames was bornd June 7th 1780, S. C. and Married November
  10th 1803, S. C.
William Andress departed this life on 30th August 1841.
Ann Andress Departed this life the 10th November 1870, Alabama
  and buried 7 miles East of Greenville, Butler County, family
  grave --------- (yard?).
They moved to Alabama the Early part of 1819. They Raised nine
  children - Susannah, Sarah Ann, Martha, Mary, Jeremiah,
  Joseph, John N., W. J. Andress, S. F. Andress.

BIRTHS:
Stephen F. Andress was bornd 22 the year of 1824 borned Monroe
  County, Ala.
Sarah J. East was born March the 8th in the year of 1827 Monroe
  County, Ala., and was married on the 25 of January 1849 in
  Lowndes County Ala.
Francis Marion Andress was (illegible) November 1st and in the
  year of Our Lorde 1849   7 miles East of Greenville, Butler
  County Ala.
William Joseph Andress was borned September 21 and in the year
  of Our Lord 1851 - 7 mile East Greenville B.C. (Butler Co.)
  Ala.
Samuel Ivy Andress was borned on April 25 and in the year of Our
Lord 1853 - 7 mile East Greenville B. C. Ala.
Nancy Caroline Andress and Elizabeth Victory Andress was borned
July the 18th in the year of Our Lord 1855 - B. C. Ala.
Mary Ann Andress was borned August the 19th and in the year of
  Our Lord 1857 - B. C. Ala.
Sarah Emily Andress was borned August the 1st in the year of Our
  Lord 1859 - B. C. Ala.
Stephen Davis Andress was borned May the 11th and in the year of
  our Lorde 1861 - B. C. Alabama
Mandy Lou Andress was borned February the 14 day of August Lorde
  1866 - B C (Butler County).
Alabama Andress was borned April 29 day in the year of Our
  Lorde 1868 - B. C. Ala
John Lee Andress was borned January the 3rd Day of the year
  1870 - 7 miles East Greenville Butler County Ala

DEATHS:
Nancy Caroline Andress departed This Life on the 14th day of
  March in the year of Our Lord 1857 - B. C. Ala
Samuel Ivey Andress departed this Life on the 24 day of September
  in the year of Our Lord 1863 - B. C. Ala
Stephen Davis Andress departed this Life on the 29th day of
  September our Lorde 1863 - B. C. Ala
Alabama Andress departed this Life on the 15 day of September
  in the year of Our Lord 1872 - B. C. Ala
Mary Ann Barrett departed this life on the 8th day of January
  1868 Butler Co Ala
Sarah E. Barrett departed this life on the 13th day of April
  1899 Butler Co Ala
  (Continued).

Stephen F. Andress departed this life on the 25th day of
April 1908, Butler Co Ala
Sarah J. (illegible) departed this life on the 25th day of
March 1909, Butler Co Ala
Francis Marion Andress departed this life on the 10th day of
September A.D. 1923. Butler Co Ala

JEREMIAH ANDRESS * Bible

A Zerox copy of the original in possession of Mrs. John W. Curtis,
Eufaula, Ala.

BIRTHS:
Jeremiah Andress borned January 28th, 1809.
Sarah Ann Banister born January the 18th, 1818.

The names and births of the children of the above parents:
Susanna Andress borned February the 7th, 1833.
John J. Andress borned August the 15th 1834.
Marion J. Andress borned July the 29th 1836.
William S. Andress borned May the 22nd, 1839.
Sarah Ann Andress borned October the 6th (?) 1840.
Mary Frances Andress borned April the 22nd, 1842.
Joseph Andress borned December the 7th, 1844.
Norah Cath Andress borned January the 16th, 1847.
Thomas J. K.(?) Andress borned January 12th, 1849.
Dorcas Andress borned September the 16th, 1850.
Jackson Andress borned May the 21st, 1852.
Nancy Andress borned November the 15, 1854.
1st Samuel Banister Andress May the 30. 1856.
Jorge H. Andress April the 3, 1859.
Martha E. Andress January 6, 1861.
2nd Samuel B. Andress was borned the 18th in the year 1863.

MARRIAGES:
Jeremiah Andress and Sarah Banister, Dec the 3rd 1831.
Shesannah (Susanna?) Andress and R. M. C. Pollard was married
the 20th July 1851.
John J. Andress and Julia A. Mosly was married Nov. 12th 1858.
William S. Andress and Rebecca F. Sims was married March 13th 1862.
Joseph S. Andress and R. F. Andress, wife of W. S. Andress, was
married Dec. the 21st, 1865.
Thomas J. Andress and Mane (illegible) McQueen was married the
18 day of Nov. 1875.

DEATHS:
Mary Frances Andress, October 27th, 1847.
Dorcas Andress departed this life July 26, 1851.
Nancy Andress departed this life June 20 1855
Samuel Banister Andress departed this life October the 14 1841
Marion J. Andress departed this life December the 25, 1841.
James J. Andress Departed this life November the 20th 1862.(Cont.)

* Typed at bottom of page: Family Bible of Jeremiah Andress,
Grand Son of Joseph Andress.

JEREMIAH ANDRESS Bible continued:

Sarah Andress Wife of J. Andress Departed this life Sep.
   30th, 1863.
Lanorah C. Andress Departed this Life Sep. 3rd 1863.
William J. Andress Departed this life Nov. 28th 1864 - Battle
   field Franklin, Tennsee.
Jorge H. Andress Departed this Life Oct. 18th 1873.

MCKINZIE and GOODSON Bible Records
Owned by Mrs. John W. Curtis, Eufaula, Ala.

BIRTHS:
Mary Goodson the Daughter of James Goodson and Jane his wife was
   born August 9th 1792. (Note: Jas. Goodson, Rev. Soldier).
Lusinda McKinzie the daughter of John McKinzie and Mary his wife
   was born April 3rd 1814
Elias G. McKinzie the son of John McKinzie and Mary his wife was
   born April 29th 1815
Mary Ann McKinzie the daughter of John McKinzie and Mary his wife
   was born ..... 7th 1816.
James Henry McKinzie the son of John McKinzie and Mary his wife
   was born January 11th 1817
Senthey Jane McKinzie the daughter of John McKinzie and his wife
   Mary was born May 39th 1818
John McKinzie the son of John McKinzie and Mary his wife was
   born March 19th 1820.
Dianna McKinzie the daughter of John McKinzie and Mary his wife
   was born 1821
Charles McKinzie the son of John McKinzie and Mary his wife was
   born July 11th 1822
Melvina McKinzie the daughter of John McKinzie and Mary his wife
   was born January 15th 1824
Monervia McKinzie the daughter of John McKinzie and his wife
   Mary was born December 27, 1825
Roderick McKinzie the son of John McKinzie and Mary his wife
   was born May 7th 1827
Harriett Catherine McKinzie the daughter of John McKinzie and
   Mary his wife was born January 11th 1829
William Goodson Tipton McKinzie the son of John McKinzie and
   Mary his wife was born Feb. 19th 1831
Polly Jane McKinzie the daughter of John McKinzie and his wife
   Mary was born May 4th 1833

MCKENZIE - HARRISON Records
Owned by Mrs. John W. Curtis, Eufaula, Ala. (Loose pages from Bi*
of John Thomas McKenzie and Sarah Melvina Harrison).

John Thomas McKenzie was born April 8, 1843 - Butler Co., Ala.
Sarah Melvina Harrison was born Sept. 8, 1845, Butler Co., Ala.
John T. McKenzie and Sarah M. Harrison were married on 21st of
   December 1866, Butler County, Alabama.

THEIR CHILDREN:
   (Continued).

Nancy Elizabeth McKenzie born Nov. 16, 1867
William Elias McKenzie born Nov. 4, 1869.
Moses James McKenzie born Nov. 29, 1871
John Thomas McKenzie, (Jr.) born Nov. 1873.
Mary Ellen McKenzie born Sept. 10th 1876.
Sarah Melvina McKenzie born May 27, 1881.
Charlie Carr McKenzie born August 15, 1883.
Kathryn Isobel McKenzie born July 10, 1886. (Katie Belle).
Rosa Harrison McKenzie born Oct. 2, 1889.

MARRIAGES:
James K. McKenzie and Mary Shirling were married 2 Dec. 1870.
William S. Harrison and _____ McKenzie were married
    August 22, 1872.
W. E. McKenzie and Emer Herbert were married ......23, 1872.
Tom Morgan and I. D. Harrison were married May 2, 1861.

DEATHS:
John Thomas McKenzie, (Sr.) died June 3, 1926, Selma, Ala. (Note:
    buried in Fort Deposit Ala. Cemetery).
Sarah Melvina H. McKenzie died August 15, 1914, Selma, Ala.
    (Buried in Fort Deposit Alabama Cemetery).
Rosa Harrison McKenzie died May 1954.

WILSON Bible
Owned by Mrs. R. Earl Wilson, Eufaula, Ala.

MARRIAGES:
This is to Certify that Thomas Minchew Wilson and Mary Jane Frost
    were solemnly United by me in Holy Matrimony at Forney *, Ala
    on the 23rd day of Oct. In the Year of Our Lord One Thousand
    Eight Teen hundred and Sixty Two. In the Presence of J. M.
    Canfield.
H. V. Shaw & Matilda Wilson Nov. 13th 1884.
W. M. Wilson & Mary F. Shaw Dec 31st. 1885
James M. Wilson & Adella Hester Dec. 21st 1890
Arthur D. Wilson & Sallie E. Minton Dec 27th 1899.
Family Record of A. D. Wilson
Arthur D. Wilson & Sarah E. Minton Dec. 27, 1899 (Duplicate).
Floyd Shelton & Alta Doss (No date).
Thelma & J. L. Snead, September 9, 1920
Deual Wilson & Ester White Sept. 2 1923
E. Grace (Wilson) & Mack Montgomery Dec. 15, 1935
Grace (Montgomery) & Charles Fleming Sept. 3, 1938
Catherine (Wilson) & Frank West Nov. 9, 1927
Earl Wilson & Annie Gipson Calhoun Dec. 22, 1941.

BIRTHS:
Thomas M. Wilson Dec. 28th 1845
Mary J. Wilson Jan 6th 1846
John Dyar P. Wilson Aug 24th 1863 (at) Forney Ala *
William M. Wilson Feb. 22nd 1866
Joice Matilda Wilson Apr. 15 1868
James M. Wilson Apr. 19th 1872
Anderson Jefferson Wilson Aug 19th 1875 (Continued).

WILSON Bible continued:
Arthur D. Wilson Sept. 4th 1878
Sara E. Wilson May 25, 1881 at Bluffton, Ala *
Floyd S. Wilson Oct. 16, 1900 Forney, Ala. *
Mary T. Wilson Sept 27, 1902 Forney Ala
Deual M. Wilson Nov. 29, 1904 Forney Ala.
Robert E. Wilson Aug. 2, 1907 Forney Ala.
John A. Wilson June 1, 1910 Forney Ala.
Sarah R. Wilson Oct. 20 1912 Rock Run Ala*
Emma G. Wilson May 3, 1915 Rock Run Ala
Nell C. Wilson Dec 29, 1918 Rock Run Ala

DEATHS: (In the family of Thomas M. Wilson).
John Dyar Wilson Oct. 22 1862
Jefferson A. Wilson Feb. 6 1891
Mary J. Wilson June 8th 1916
Thomas M. Wilson July 19, 1924
William M. Wilson April 13, 1931
Mack Montgomery June 24, 1936
Matilda Wilson _____ 1936
Arthur Deuel Wilson (No date).
Duel Malcom Wilson (no date).
Mary Thelma W. Snead (no date).
Robert Earl Wilson May 22, 1964.

SNIPES Bible
Published by: Jesper Harding
No. 57 South Third Street
Philadelphia   1850

This Bible is in the possession of Mrs. J. H. Toney, Columbus, Ga.

MARRIAGES:
H. C. (Henry) Snipes and Margaret R. Cunningham were married July
   14th in the year of Our Lord 1853.
Washington P. Bass and Margaret R. Snipes were married July 28th
   in the year of Our Lord 1866.
W. O. (William Oscar) Sylvester and S. J. (Sarah Jane) Snipes wer
   married October 9th in the year of Our Lord 1873.
William H. Snipes and Margaret Stewart were married on Feb. 19th
   in the year of Our Lord 1874.
Athol R. Sylvester and Della (Alice Adella) Watson were married
   June 10, 1903.
James Herman Toney and Katherine Bernice Sylvester were married
   June 20th, 1920.
Katherine Vivian Toney and Powell Woodham were married 9-7-1947.
Henry C. Snipes was born March 25th in the year of Our Lord 1833.
Margaret R. Snipes was born 7th March in the year of Our Lord 183
William H. Snipes was born May ____ in the year of Our Lord 1854.
Sarah J. Snipes was born 2nd Jan. in the year of Our Lord 1856.
C. C. Hill was born 28th May in the year of Our Lord 1851.
(Continued).

* Forney, Bluffton and Rock Run are in Cherokee County, Alabama.

SNIPES Bible continued:
Catherine Bernice Sylvester was born May 17th, 1895.
Washington P. Bass was born 11 ------- 1840.
Rankin Augustus Bass was born 22nd May in the year 1868.
W. O. Sylvester was born Dec. 3rd 1846.
Athol Rembert Sylvester was born July 30th in the year of Our
    Lord 1875.
Demarcus A. Sylvester was born Feb. 6, 1879.
Margaret Alethae Sylvester was born 14th of May 1882.
Thomas Clifford Sylvester was born Dec. 30, 1885.

DEATHS:
Henry C. Snipes died Saturday December 11th 1858 - aged 25 years
    and 16 days.
M. B. A. Bass died Sunday morning - aged 37 years on June 1870.
William H. Snipes Died June 21, aged 52 years - 1907.
Rankin Cunningham Departed this life 28 July 1863.
Elizabeth Hill Departed this life 25 of March 1852.
Willian O. (Oscar) Sylvester Died June 16, 1909.
Sarah Jane (Snipes) Sylvester Died Feb. 22 1927 - age 71 years
    one month and 20 days.

LANE Bible

Family Bible of Charles Lane of Miller County, Georgia. Bible was
printed 1880. It is now in the possession of Mr. Charles Hance
Montgomery (son of Lou Ella E. Lane Montgomery), Port St. Joe, Fla.

DEATHS:
James T. Lane Son of Charles & E A Lane Departed This Life May
    18th 1875.
James M. Lane Departed This Life February The ------1881.
Elizabeth Lane Departed This life May The 18 1889
Charles Lane Departed This life May 26th 1906
D.A.W. Lane Departed This life May 19th 1922.
E. A. Lane Departed this life March 10, 1941 (Wife of Chas. Lane).
Henry R. Lane Departed this life March 21, 1946
Sarah D Lane Chambers died Dec. 27, 1942.
Sterling P. Lane departed   (Incomplete).
Lou Ella E. Lane Montgomery Departed this life Dec. 27, 1962.

BIRTHS:
Charles Lane Born March 2nd 1849
E. A. Lane Wife of Charles Lane Born July 11th 1855
James T. Lane Born December 16th 1873.
D.A.W. Lane Born February 21 1876.
Lou Eller E. Lane Born February 10th 1878.
Sarrah D. Lane Born April 1st 1880.
Sterling P. Lane Born January The 26th, 1882.
Frances R. Lane was Born June The 21 1884.
John B. G. Lane Born Oct. The 9th, 1886
Nancy M. Lane was Born January 12th 1889
Charley M. Lane Was Born June 15 1891
Henry R. Lane Born Nov. 11th 1894

MARRIAGES:
Charles & E A Lane Was Married December 12 1872.

MCDONALD Bible
Published by Thomas, Cowperthwait & Co.
Philadelphia - 1850

The Bible originally belonged to Dougald P. McDonald who lived in Berrien County, Ga. It is now owned by Mrs. Geo. M. Carson, Atlanta, Ga.

BIRTHS:
Mary Virginia McDonald daughter of D. P. McDonald and Elizabeth Jane his wife was born June 2nd AD 1852.
Wm. Alexander McDonald son of D. P. McDonald and Elizabeth Jane his wife, was born July 15th AD 1853.
Lucien Adolphus McDonald son of D. P. McDonald & E. Jane his wife was born March 31st 1855.
Jas. Marshal McDonald son of D. P. McDonald & Elizabeth Jane his wife was born June 22nd 1859.
Jefferson D. McDonald Son of D. P. McDonald & Elizabeth Jane his wife was born Saturday June 15th 1861.
Maggie Melissa McDonald daughter of D. P. McDonald & J. J. McDona his wife was born Thursday 16th July 1863.
Dugald Howard Whitington Son of B. F. Whitington and M. Virginia his wife was born April 1st 1888.
Beulah Augusta Whittington daughter of B. F. Whittington and Mary Virginia his wife was born Nov. 21st 1868.
Benjamin Eugene Whittington Son of B. F. Whittington and Mary Virginia his wife was born Feb. 23d 1871.
Lilla McDonald Whittington daughter of B. F. Whittington and Mary Virginia his wife was born January 24th 1874.
Mabel Whittington Daughter of B. F. Whittington & M. Virginia his wife was born November 18th 1883.
Clarence Whittington Son of B. F. Whittington & M. Virginia his wife was born March 14th 1877.
Cora Whittington Daughter of B. F. Whittington & M. Virginia his wife was born November 15th 1879.
Ethel Whittington Daughter of B. F. Whittington and M. Virginia his wife was born Sept 23d, 1881.
Matie McDougald (or McDonald?) Whittington Daughter B. F. Whittington & M. Virginia His wife was born September 18th 1885.

DEATHS:
Elizabeth J. McDonald wife of D. P. McDonald died Tuesday June 18 1861 - aged 26 years 4 months & 23 days.
Jefferson D. McDonald died Monday 2nd day of Augt. 1861, aged 1 month & 17 days.
D. P. McDonald died Sunday Evening May 27th 1866 in the 43rd year of his age.
Mary Virginia McD. Whittington Died July 16, 1926
B. F. Whittington born Nov. 8, 1840 Died Nov. 4 1922
Cora Whittington died July 20th 1881.
Mabel Whittington died January 12th 1884.
Dougal Howard Whittington died June 22nd 1889.
Lilla McD. W. Pinkston wife of J. W. Pinkston, Sr. March 11 (?) Died 1918.
Clarence Whittington Died Dec. 22 1944
Ethel Whittington died Jan 25, 1935.
(Continued).

MCDONALD Bible continued:

MARRIAGES:
B. F. Whittington & M. V. McDonald Married Nov. 10th 1867
D. P. McDonald & J. A. J. Peeples Married Nov. 26th 1861

BIRTHS:
Marguerite Virginia, Daughter of B. F. Whittington and M. Virginia his Wife was born December 25th 1890.
Marion Elizabeth Daughter of B. F. Whittington & M. Virginia his wife was born May 4th 1893.

CHARLES DUNNING Bible
Owned by Mrs. Walter C. Miller, Eufaula, Alabama

MARRIAGES:
Charles Dunning married to Elizabeth Ann Dorsey Octr 30th 1823
Thomas Miller to Jane C. Dunning Jany 22nd 1843
Thomas Miller married to P. R. Lowe October the 28 1846
Thomas Miller to Susan Hillman May the 1st 1860
George Boynton to Mary Miller Dec the 6th 1871.
John W. Whittle to Lottie Miller Dec. the 15 74 (1874?).

BIRTHS:
Charles Dunning Born 12th March 1799
Elizabeth Ann Dunning Born Octr 3rd 1805
John D. Dunning Born August 18th 1824
George W. Dunning Born Octr 28th 1825
Jane Caswell Dunning Born July 23rd 1827
Mathew John Caswell Miller Born March 2nd 1844
Mary M. Lowe was Born September 19 1859
Mathew Dorsey Born July 19 1781
Elizabeth Ann Dorsey Born Octr 3rd 18 5 (1805?)
John Dorsey Born Feb 10 1791
Jane Dorsey Born July 13 1811
Nancy Dorsey Born May 22 1813
Rebecca Dorsey Born Dec. 11 1816
Easter Miller was Born Febuary 22 18, 2 (Note: As recorded).
Lottie Miller was born June the 9 1852
Reuben J. Key was born June 22 1855
J. M. Dorsey was born Nov. 30th 1844
H. A. Dorsey was born Sept 2nd 1846
Thomas Miller was born April the 17 1818
P. R. Miller was born June the 1 1832.
daughter Mary J. Miller was born July the 1 1849
daughter Lottie A. Miller was born June the 9 1852.
son Thomas D. Miller was born Decm the 1. 1854
daughter Anola Miller was born June the 1 1857
son Willie E. Miller was born Sep the 27 1859

DEATHS:
Jane Caswell Miller Died March 2nd 1844
John Dorsey Dunning Died October 6th 1845
George W Dunning Died February 8th 1848
Elizabeth A. Dunning was Born Oct 3rd 18 5 died Dec 1st 1883
Isabella Dorsey Died April 6th 1836.
(Continued).

CHARLES DUNNING BIBLE continued:
Nancy Sims Died March 5th 1847.
Jane Glenn Died August 6 1858
Mathew Dorsey Died Ocllober (October) 22 1861
Mathew J. C. Miller died May 20 1862 in his 19th year
Easter Miller died Octtober (October) 27 1867 in her sixty
   six year
Thomas Miller died Feb the 13 1862.
P. R. Miller died Jan the 21 1860.
John Dorsey Died Sept 18, 1867

JOHN HENRY LEWIS Bible
Owned by Mrs. Walter C. Miller, Eufaula, Alabama.
MARRIAGES:
John Henry Lewis & Martha Ann Dunning was married by Rev. Joseph
   T. Turman April 9th 1855
William Gabriel Lewis Married Mittie Mae Espy 12/17/1891
   Their children:
   John Allen Lewis born Mar. 6, 1893
   Elizabeth Espy Lewis born May 12 1894
   William Roy Lewis born Dec. 20 1895
   Seaborn Joseph Lewis born July 17 1898
   Edgar Gabriel & Ethel Mae Lewis (twins) born May 24 1901.
Seaborn Joseph Lewis married Helen Nason Feb 9 1923
   Their daughter:
   Jo-Ellen Lewis born June 9, 1924.
Ethel Mae Lewis married Walter C. Miller Aug. 26, 1945.
Mary C. Lewis married Henry Beverette Jan. 21 1894 by
   Rev. Philoman C. Harris.
BIRTHS:
Matthew Small Hightower was born in the year of our Lord
   Jan 9 1800
Mary Hightower born Mar 5 1804
William Capers Hightower was born Aug 6 1822
Matthew Sanford Hightower was born May 8 1824
Gabriel Lewis was born May 22nd 1785
Obodiah Richard Lewis was born Nov 2 1828
John Henry Lewis was born July 20 1831
Susan Elizabeth Lewis was born June 13th 1833
Annie Brown Lewis was born Mar 10th 1835
Gabriel Walker Lewis was born Feb 4th 1837
Mary Corrine Lewis was born A D Feb. 18th 1858
William Gabriel Lewis was born A D March 5th 1860
John Henry Lewis was born in the year of our Lord March 9 1862
Mary Corrine & William Gabriel Lewis was Holy Consecrated to the
   Lord by N. E. Boland June 2nd 1863
John Henry Lewis was dedicated to the Lord by Holy Baptism
   August 15 1867
Martha Eva Pearl Beverette was born AD Oct. 21st· 1898 and was
   consecrated to the Lord at "Camp McGhee" camp meeting in 1898
Mattie Eva Pearl Beverette joined the M. E. Church of Cuthbert
   A D 1907.

   (Continued).

JOHN HENRY LEWIS Bible continued:
DEATHS:
John H. Lewis departed this life July 22 1864
Mrs. Martha A. Lewis departed this life March 19th 1923.
William Gabriel Lewis died 12-26-35.
Mittie Espy Lewis died Jan. 1, 1947.
John A. (Henry) Lewis died July 18, 1929.
Elizabeth Espy Lewis died Mar. 13, 1955.
William Roy Lewis died Mar. 1st 1950.
Edgar Lewis died Oct. 14, 1902.
Seaborn Joseph Lewis died Apr. 19, 1968.

WILLIAM WRIGHT FAULK Bible
Owned by Mrs. Sara Ethridge Ross, Birmingham, Ala.

Barbour Co.
BIRTHS:
H. L. Faulk was borned Nov. 24th 1813.
S. J. Faulk was borned Jan. 14th 1823.
W. W. Faulk was borned Aug. 26th 1846.
Henry Bennett Faulk was borned Nov. 29th 1848.
James Harrison Faulk was borned Nov. 18th 1850.
Mary Jane Faulk was borned Feb. 1st, 1853.
Leonora Alabama Faulk March 27th 1855.
Nancy Elizabeth Faulk May 16th 1857.
Charlott Ann Jemima Faulk was borned April 4th 1859.
Jefferson Davis Faulk was borned June 13th 1861.
Rozell Faulk was borned Oct. 3, 1876.
W. H. Faulk was Bornd Aug. 22, 1848.
Cornelius C. Norwood born May 12, 1857.
Jessie Norwood born July 12, 1891.
Lawson Cornelius Norwood Sept. 26, 1892.
Alexander Stephens Norwood Aug. 11, 1894.
Atticus Haygood Norwood June 20, 1897.

Barbour Co. Family Record of William Wright and Sarah Jane Faulk
BIRTHS:
W. W. Faulk was borned Aug. 26th 1846.
Sarah Jane Faulk was borned June 22nd 1854.
Cora Faulk was borned Sept. 8th 1877.
Leonora Faulk was borned June 14th 1879.
A. L. McLean borned April 13, 1874.
William Shirley Ethridge was borned April the 19th, 1903, Died
    May 3, 1957.
W. W. Ethridge was borned Oct. 3, 1867, Died Sept. 17, 1948.
Sarah Jane Ethridge was borned May 27th 1906.
Leonora Wright Ethridge was borned March 11, 1908, Died June 3,
    1950.
J. N. Stephens borned Mar. 2, 1873.
Charles James Dudley Borned Feb. 18, 1909.
Charles James Dudley, Jr. Borned July 1, 1933.
Harold William Ross Borned March 20, 1901.
Olene S. Ethridge Oct. 18, 1907.
Larry Charles Dudley Jan. 18, 1960.
David Glenn Dudley Feb. 21, 1961.
Etta Jean Moore Dudley Feb. 21, 1934.
Michael Dean Dudley Nov. 11, 1966.
(Continued).

WILLIAM WRIGHT FAULK Bible continued:
DEATHS:
Nancy Elizabeth Faulk Died June 23, 1862.
Sarah Jane Faulk wife of H. L. Faulk Died April 24th 1864
H. L. Faulk Died July 27th 1870
Leonora A. Faulk Died May 2nd, 1879.
Rozell Faulk Died Feb. 13th 1883.
J. D. Faulk Died Aug. 9th 1883.
J. H. Faulk Died Jan. 15, 1885.
H. B. Faulk died Dec. 1907.
Mary Jane Faulk Died May 15, 1930.
A. L. McLean Died Feb. 28th 1933.
Cornelius C. Norwood died April 22, 1911.
Sarah Jane Faulk wife of W. W. Faulk Died Aug. 9th, 1886.
William Wright Faulk died March 1st, 1908.
W. H. Faulk Died Nov. 25, 1943.
Charlotte Faulk Norwood Died Oct. 11, 1947.
William Wesley Ethridge Died September 17, 1948 (Friday morning).
Leonora E. Dudley June 3, 1950.
Jane Nelson Stephens Oct. 11, 1949 died Tuesday buried Thursday.
William Shirley Ethridge Died May 3, 1957.
Cora Faulk Ethridge wife of Will Ethridge died Jan. 19, 1971.

FAMILY RECORD:
Henry Lawson and Sarah Jane Faulk nee Bizzell:
MARRIAGES:
H. L. Faulk and S. J. Faulk was married June 29th 1845.
W. H. Faulk and M. J. Faulk was Married Dec. 23, 1875.
C. C. Norwood and Charlotte Ann Faulk married Sept. 1890.
Homer Hall and Jessie Norwood married July 5, 1923.
Lawson C. Norwood and Flora Mae Woods married June 1, 1938.
W. W. Faulk and Sarah Jane Faulk Married Nov. 28th 1876.
A. L. McLean and Nora Faulk was Married June 16, 1901.
W. W. Ethridge and Cora Faulk was Married June 19, 1902.
Charlie James Dudley and Leonora Wright Ethridge was Married
    Aug. 12, 1932.
J. N. Stephens and Nora Faulk McLean married Feb. 24th 1937.
Harold William Ross and Sara Jane Ethridge married Jan. 23, 1945.
William Shirley Ethridge   Olene Stephens O'Conner   Troy Ala.
    April 19, 1952.

The following outline of the Faulk family given by Mrs. Ross:
Henry Lawson Faulk married Sarah Jane Bizell. Issue:
    William Wright Faulk
    Henry Bennett Faulk
    James Harrison Faulk
    Mary Jane Faulk
    Leonora Faulk
    Nancy Elizabeth Faulk
    Charlotte Ann Jemima Faulk
    Jefferson Davis Faulk

William Wright Faulk married Sarah Jane Faulk. Issue:
    Cora and twin brother
    Leonora Faulk

Mary Jane Faulk married William Henry Faulk. Issue:
    Rozelle Faulk
    (Continued).

Cornelius Cincinnatus Norwood married Charlotte Ann
    Jemima Faulk. Issue:
    Jessie Norwood
    Lawson Cornelius Norwood
    Atticus Haygood Norwood
Henry Bennett Faulk married Mae Waddell. Issue:
    Frances Jane Faulk.

HARDWICK Bible
Owned by Miss Emma Lucy Hardwick, Abbeville, Henry Co., Ala.
MARRIAGES:
Capt. Marion C. J. Searcy and Lucy A. Richards was married
    Sept. 24th 1863
2nd marriage:
Col. Wm. Hardwick and Lucy A. Searcy was Married January 5th 1868
R. E. Richards & Roann Craddock married December 13th 1855.
BIRTHS:
Thomas Marion Searcy was borned June 27th 1864
Robert Lee Hardwick was borned April 25th 1869.
George Franklin Oscar Hardwick was borned 16th May 1870
Jas. Clanton Hardwick was borned 7th July 1871
Watt Carter Hardwick was borned Nov. 21 1873
Nina Corine Hardwick was borned Sept. 15th 1876
Eddie Mack Harwick was borned Jan 11th 1879
Mattie Estell and Maggie Elouise Hardwick was borned Oct. 4th 1880
Lucy Jane Hardwick was bornd Jun 22nd 1883
Dan Gordon Hardwick was borned August 31th 1885
Thomas Richards was bornd Sept 14th 1798.
Thos. Hinton Richards was born Sept 6th 1857.

DEATHS:
Roon R. Richards Died Sept 16th AD 1857
Robt. E. Richards Killed in war Jan 5th 1863
R. F. Richards Killed in war Sept 15th 1863
Thos Richards Died June 25th 1879
Capt. Marion C. J. Searcy Died In war Dec. 9, 1863
Maggie Elouise Hardwick Died Sept 3/ 1881
Mattie Estell Hardwick Died Sept 24, 1881

Loose page in Bible:
W. C. Hardwick married Miss M. L. (Mamie Leila) Herndon
    15 Dec 1895

HAYGOOD Bible
Owned by Mr. Hasting Vann Owens, Abbeville, Henry Co., Ala.
Presented to Miss M. E. Haygood by her Brother - October the
    24th /58 - A. W. Haygood.
Death date included in the Bible - written on a card:
W. A. Haygood Died Oct. 18, 1888 Aged 51 years, 3 months.
BIRTHS:
H. E. Owens was born Sept 8th 1817.
Frances Jane Stuart was born Sept 23rd 1823.
(Continued).

HAYGOOD Bible continued:
Mary E. Haygood was born Sept 5th 1839.
Ann Elfreda, daughter of Hasting E. & Frances J. Owens, was born Decr. 20rd 1849.
Edwin Hickson, son of Hasting E. & Frances J. Owens, was born Decr. 28th 1851
Helen Robinson, daughter of Hasting E. & Frances J. Owens, was born March 21st 1854.
Millard Filmore, son of Hasting E. & Frances J. Owens, was born October 20th 1855.
Gustave Beauregard, son of H. E. & F. J. Owens, was born 17 July 1859.
Thaddeus Bennett, son of Hasting E. & Mary E. (Note: Mary E. Haygood - 2nd wife) Owens, was born May 20th 1862.
Hasting Whitman, son of Hasting E. & Mary E. Owens, was born March 26th 1872.
Nettie Owens, daughter of Edwin Hickson & Lelia H. (Note: Simonton) Owens and grand-daughter of Hasting E. Owens, was born March 4th 1874.
Mary Vann, wife of H. W. Owens, was born March 17, 1873.
Hasting Vann, son of H. W. & Mary Vann Owens, was born Dec. 4, 1899

MARRIAGES:
Hasting E. Owens and Frances Jane Stuart were married Decr. 15th AD 1847
Hasting E. Owens and Mary E. Haygood were married Decr. 1st 1869.

DEATHS:
James Whitman, son of Hasting E. & Frances J. Owens, died May 30th 1850
Ann Elfreda, daughter of Hasting E. & Frances J. Owens, died March 12th 1856
Thaddeus Bennett, son of Hasting E. & Frances J. Owens, died July 22nd 1862.
Millard F. Owens, son of Hasting & Frances J. Owens, died near Macon, Ga. Sept 11th 1883.
Frances Jane Owens, wife of Hasting E. Owens, died January 31st 1868.
Hasting E. Owens died November 18th 1895, at his home in Abbeville, Alabama
Mary E. Owens, wife of Hasting E. Owens, died April 8th 1901 in Pinckard Alabama
Hasting Whitman Owens died March 15th 1933 at about 10 A.M. in the Probate Office of Henry County, Ala.
James Robert Owens died December 24, 1935 at about 1:30 P. M. in Abbeville Alabama.
Mary V. Owens died 11th 1940 about 8:45 A.M. in Abbeville, Alabama

---

AVENT - MCLENDON Bible
Owned by Col. John McLendon, Cottonton, Russell County, Ala.
MARRIAGES:
Enoch W. McLendon & Lilla May, February 14, 1893 (at) Loflin, Russell Co., Ala.
Charles H. McLendon & Kate Mathis b. May 31, 1917, married (Continued).

AVENT - MCLENDON Bible continued:
   August 22, 1953 Opelika, Lee County, Ala.
Child: Joan Charlendon b. Aug. 9, 1955 - Columbus, Ga.

John Calvin McLendon & Katharine Elizabeth Pyle b. Oct. 10, 1919 -
   Kingsport, Tenn. - married May 4, 1939 - Marion Va.
Child: Jane Wall McLendon b. Feb. 18, 1943 - Kingsport, Tenn.

BIRTHS:
Enoch Washington McLendon Aug. 29, 1856
Lilla May McLendon Feb. 12, 1870.
Children:
   Wilton McLendon, Dec. 11, 1893
   Charles Hatten McLendon, Dec. 25, 1895
   Lilla May McLendon, Mar. 27, 1898
   Rosa Lee McLendon, Feb. 21, 1900
   John Calvin McLendon, Aug. 13, 1906   E. W. McLendon, Jr. Nov. 16, 1903.

DEATHS:
Wilton McLendon, Dec. 14, 1896
Enoch W. McLendon, Aug. 13, 1927
Lilla May McLendon, Sept. 28, 1938

(Note: Bible was presented to Mary L. Avent by W. F. Avent on Jany 12, 1889. The Avents had no children - distantly related to the McLendon family. In back of the Bible:.........in loving Remembrance of Mrs. W. W. Maples- Died Sept. 14 1888).

MAY Bible
Owned by Mrs. M. C. McLendon, Cottonton, Russell County, Ala.

BIRTHS:
Georgia Ann Powell was born Sept. 18th 1848.
Fannie Powell was born July 18th 1850.
Lilla May was born Feb. 12th 1870.
Johnnie Calvin May was born Sept. 18th 1880.
Charles Whitaker May was born Sept 9th 1883.
Georgia Annie May was born Aug. 25th 1886.
Marie May was born Dec. 25th 1889.
Louise May was born Sept. 22nd 1892.
Mr. John May was born Oct. 5, 1844.

MARRIAGES:
Georgia Ann Powell was married to Mr. John May Oct. 23rd 1868.
Fannie Powell was married to Mr. John May Dec. 19th 1879.
Mr. John May was married Dec. 19th 1879 (Note: different hand writing.).

DEATHS:
Georgia May, wife of Mr. John May died Dec. 22nd 1870.
Charles May, Son of John May died March 21, 1904.
Fannie Powell wife of John May died June 14, 1908, 10:30.

RAMBO Bible
Owned by Mrs. Leckie Mattox, Eufaula, Ala.

On the first page of the New Testament is written: Preston A. Rambo
   (Continued).

son of M. & E. C. Rambo died July 13, 1946 at home in Petropolis, buried in Brazil.

BIRTHS:
Mary (Adams) Rambo the mother of Daniel Rambo was born & died in Edgefield, S.C.- She was the wife of Laurence Rambo - They le two sons, Daniel & Sam. Rambo.
Mary (Adams) Rambo is the mother of Daniel Rambo and Mary (Jackso Rambo was Daniel's grandmother. Both husbands named Laurence Rambo - Jan. 1938 by Regina Rambo Murph.
Daniel Rambo was born the 14th day of February 1785 in South Carolina Edgefield District - November the 28th 1847.
Jane W. Rambo wife of Daniel Rambo was born Dec. 6th 1790.
Eliza S. Rambo was born March 24th 1814.
Thurza L. Rambo was born August 29th 1816.
Christian C. Rambo was born August 29th 1819.
Samuel Rambo was born January 24th 1818.
Mary Fort Rambo was born September 4th 1821.
Wesley Rambo was born February 12th 1823.
Drury Rambo was born May 9th 1824.
Fielding Rambo was born October 28th 1825.
Henrietta Rambo was born February 1st 1827.
Jane Rambo was born November 8th 1828.
Marcellus Rambo was born May 17th 1830.

BIRTHS:
Jno. DeG. son of Christopher & Hannah Sartor was born Aug. 29th 1796.
Nancy Collier wife of John DeG. (deGraffenried) was born March 18
Joseph Treyvante son of John & Nancy deG was born Jan. 1st 1823.
Regina, daughter of John & Nancy deG was born dec the 30th 1826 3 o'clock P.M., aged 13 yrs old when her mother died.
Henrietta daughter of Jno. deG & Nancy was born Oct. 31 1828, 7 o'clock P.M.
J. C. deG son of Jno & Nancy deG was born Nov. 12th 1830 between 11 & 12 o'clock A.M.
C. Teacharner son of Jno. & Nancy deG was born April 23 - 1833
Spicer P.(or F.) son of Jno. & Nancy deG was born Aug. 4th 1835 10 P.M.
Francis Hobson son of Jno. & Nancy deG was born Jan. 17th 1837 11 P.M.

Family of D. G. & Lillian Goodwin
Drury deG. Jr. son born Oct. 3, 1921.
(Note: the following entries were at the top of the next page):
Mollie McCaskill Rambo b. May 29, 1849 in Marshallville, Ga.
Edith Murph dau. of Burke & Regina Murph born Feb. 10, 1916 at home in Marshallville at 3 P. M.
Ignatius Few Murph son of Burke & Regina Murph born June 15, 191? Saturday at 6 P.M.
Ruth Murph dau. of Burke & Regina Murph born April 19, 1923 at 1 P.M.
Nancy Lynn Randolph daughter of R. H. & Edith Murph Randolph born in Marine Hospital, Stapleton, S. I., N. Y. on Sept. 13, 194?
Sandra Lee Randolph dau. of R. H. & Edith Murph Randolph born in St. Mary's Hospital in Athens, Ga. Sept. 27, 1944.
(Continued).

RAMBO Bible continued:

Drury Rambo family record.
BIRTHS:
Drury Rambo was born May 9th 1824.
Regina Rambo wife of Drury Rambo was born December 30th 1826.
John Daniel Rambo was born November 28th 1846.
Ann Eliza Rambo was born July 13th, 1848.
Christopher Techarner Rambo was born August 9th 1850.
Drury Baker Rambo was born March 3d, 1852.
Regina Henrietta Rambo was born Sept 4th 1853.
Jane Olivia Rambo was born August 1st 1855.
Lawrence Wesley Rambo was born Nov. 2d, 1859.
Mary Hobson Rambo was born Dec. 10th 1857.

Drury deGraffenried Rambo was born Sept. 25th 1862, Thursday

Jno. D. Rambo's family record
Mollie McCaskill born May 29, 1849.
Laurence McCaskill Rambo was born Sept. 20th 1878.
Willie Vida Rambo was born 15th October 1879.
Ermine deG Rambo was born 1st Jan 1884.

Lila Hattaway Rambo wife of Laurence M. Rambo born (Incomplete).
Ellen Rambo daughter of Laurence & Lila Born Jan. 5th 1908.
Jane, daughter of Laurence & Lila Rambo born March 28 - 1911
Laurence Marcellus Rambo son of L. & L. born   19--
Judith Rambo daughter of Laurence & Lila born Nov. 4, 1919.

Sam'l Rambo's family
BIRTHS:
Infant son of S. & E. Rambo was born -/43 & died 4 hours old.
Ella Rambo daughter of Saml & Elizabeth (Fort) Rambo was born
Elizabeth, daughter of Saml. & Elizabeth (Fort) Rambo was born on
    July 23d, 1846.
Adelle daughter of Saml. & Lydia (Fort) Rambo was born 20th
    Sept. 1848.
Albert Murray son of Saml. & Lydia (Fort) Rambo was born
    Aug. 2d, 1850.
George Givhan son of Saml & Lydia (Fort) Rambo 29th Oct. 1854.
Louis Hazelius   son of Saml & Lydia Rambo was born Sept.
    27th 1857.

Family of Ermine   & W. E. Watkins
Mollie deG, daughter of Ermine   & W. E. Watkins was born
    Jan. 24, 1911.
A Son born ---- 19

John D. Rambo, Jr., son of Florence Childs & J. D. Rambo born
    Jan. 24, 1926 in Macon, Ga.
William Wimberly Rambo son of Florence & J. D. born July 12, 1930
    in Macon, Ga.

M. Rambo's family
(Continued).

BIRTHS:
Charley Lenox Son of Marcellus and E. C. Rambo was born
   8th Jan. 1851, Died Sept. 17, 1926.
J. W. Rambo daughter of Marcellus & E. C. Rambo was born May 31,
   1852, Died Jan. 21, 1890, Married Ed Williams of Oglethorpe,
Samuel Dillard, son of M. & E. C. Rambo was born June 29th 1855,
   Died in Marietta, Ga. Nov. 3, 1933.
Thomas Albert son of M. & E. C. Rambo was born Dec. 16th 1859,
   Died Oct. 29, 1880.
Preston Ambrose Rambo born Nov. 8, 1866, Died July 13, 1946.

Family of Willie Vida Rambo Murph and John Speight Murph:
Infant daughter of John & W. V. born & died May (Incomplete).
Mollie Irene Murph born April 18, 1912, daughter of W. V. & John
   Murph.
John Speight, Jr., son of W. V. & John Murph born Jan. 2, 1919.

Written by   Mother   6/29/1918
William Berrien Hattaway III, son of Florence Rambo Hattaway &
   William Berrien Hattaway, Jr., was born June 7th 1918 in
   Bluffton, Ga.
Dorothy Hattaway, daughter of Florence & Will, born May 20th 1926
   in Bluffton, Ga. at Fairfield Farm.
Wm. Hattaway Brantley born Nov. 25, 1940 in Troy, Ala.
Jill Rambo Brantley born Aug. 5, 1943.

John L. & H.   McElvin's family
BIRTHS:
Thirza J. McElven daughter of J. L. & H. McE. was born Oct. 30,
   1845.
Wm. J. McElven was born 21st March 1848.
Ermine S. McElven was born Dec. 5th, 1850.
Drury R. McElven was born Nov. 11th, 1852.
Jno. L. McElven, Jun was born Dec. 10th 1857.
Clara G. McElven was born May 3d, 1859.
Regina H. McElven was born Aug. 7th 1856 and died when 2 years o]

Family of Ann Edith Rambo Baldwin & Robert Edwin Baldwin Senior:
Clara Lillian, daughter, born Mar. 16, 1916.
Robert Edwin, Jr., son, born Aug. 11, 1921.
Betty born Nov. 4, 1923.

Family of Drury deG Rambo
BIRTHS:
Drury deGraffenried & Lillian Orr Nixon Rambo's family:
Regina deG Rambo daughter of D. deG & L. Orr Rambo was born 6th
   April 1888.
Olivia Rambo daughter of D. deG. & L. O. Rambo was born 29th
   Dec. 1889.
Drury Rambo son of D. deG. Rambo & L. O. Rambo was born on 15th
   day of January 1892.
(Note: the following entry was crossed out): John Daniel Rambo th
   son of Drury deG. & L. O. Rambo was born 25th day of April 18
Florence Rambo was born 16 March 1894.
(Continued).

RAMBO Bible continued:
John Daniel Rambo was born 25 April 1896.
Anna Edith Rambo was born 21 Dec. 1897. The last and youngest child of Drury deGraffenried Rambo & Lillian Orr Rambo - not quite 8 mos. old when her father died.

Edith Murph, daughter of Regina deG. Rambo Murph & Burke Baldwin Murph was born 10th Feb. 1916
Nash Murph, son of Regina deG. Rambo Murph & Burke B. Murph born June 15, 1918.
Ruth Murph, born April 19, 1923.

MARRIAGES:
Danl Rambo and Jane W. Fort were Married the 13th day of June 1813.
John Rudolph & Eliza Susan Rambo were married March 6th 1832.
Thirza L. Rambo & James W. McQueen were married about Sept. 1837.
H. D. Shehee & Mary Fort Rambo were Married March 24th 1842.
Samuel Rambo & Elizabeth Fort were Married September 15 1842.
John S. McElven & Henrietta Rambo were Married Jany 16th 1845.
Drury Rambo & Regina deGraffenried were Married December 18th 1845.
Marcellus Rambo & Elizabeth C. Dillard were Married April 18th 1850
Fielding Rambo & Ann Gadsden Stafford were Married July 16th 1856.
Samuel Rambo & Lydia Fort were Married Nov. 27th 1847.
John DeGraffenried & Nancy Collier were Married Aug. 1st 1822.
Jas. V. Thomas & Mary deGraffenried were married 18 oct. 1816.
Treyvant deGraf- & Rebecca C. Hill were married 1827.
J. C. deGraffenried & Elizabeth Ann Colier were Married March 22nd 1853.
J. C. deGraffenried & M. S. J. Collier were Married Dec. 25/56 (2nd wife).
C. T. deGraffenried & Laura Wooten were married (Incomplete).
Spicer F. deGraffenried & Amelia Rebecca Lunday were married September 17th 1857.
F. H. deGraffenried & Mary Emma Collier were married March 7th 1861.
John D. Rambo & Mary E. McCaskill were married Nov. 28th 1877.
Laurence McCaskill Rambo & Lila Hattaway were married August 6th 1903.
Willie Vida Rambo and John Speight Murph were married Dec. 15th, 1909.
Ermine deGraffenried Rambo and William Earnest Watkins were married Dec. 15th 1909.
(These two marriages were a double wedding at the home of their grand-father, Drury Rambo, at Bluffton, Ga.). (Written by Anna E. Rambo, their "Auntie").
Mollie Watkins married Benjamin Garland May 1936 at her home in Jackson, Ga. A lovely afternoon wedding (Sunday).
Ellen Rambo and Jack Cowart married 19--.
Jane Rambo and   married 19--.
(These two were children of Laurence & Lila Rambo).
Drury deGraffenried Rambo & Lillian Orr Nixon were married January 27th 1887.
Regina deGraffenried Rambo & Burke Baldwin Murph were married Wednesday evening Dec.   th 1912 at home of Grandfather Drury Rambo, Bluffton, Ga. (written by Olivia Rambo).
(Continued).

RAMBO Bible continued:
Florence deGraffenried Rambo and William Berrien Hattaway, Jr.
   married Wed. Dec. 20th 1916 - 6 o'clock P. M. At home
   Bluffton, Ga. (written by Olivia Rambo).
Edith Ann Rambo and Robert Edwin Baldwin were married Feb. 22nd,
   1918 - 6 o'clock P.M. at Aunt Dolly Bostwick (Mrs. W. E.
   Bostwick) at Arlington, Ga.
Drury deGraffenried Rambo & Mary Lillian Goodwin were married
   Nov. 26, 1919 (or 1920) at her home in Marshallville, Ga.
   Wednesday evening - 6 o'clock.
John Daniel Rambo & Florence Childs of Talberton, Ga. were married
   June 8, 1924 in Blakely, Ga. at parsonage by Rev. J. W. Arnold
Edith Murph and Rivington   Hammon Randolph were married Sunday
   afternoon 5 o'clock August 20th 1939 at home, five miles east
   of Marshallville, Ga. at "Wilkes Knob". Only immediate families
   present, about 50 - Rev. Harris Gillespie, Methodist Minister
   of Marshallville, performed ring ceremony.
Dorothy Hattaway and Tommy Kirven Brantley were married Dec. 27,
   1939 in the early morning. They eloped Tuesday P.M., rode all
   night & finally got a Methodist Minister at or near Gulf Port
   Miss. to tie the knot.
Wm. B. Hattaway, III and Rosalyn Kirklin of Troy, Ala. were married
   Sept. 1st, 1940 at Prattville, Ala. Twas Sunday night that they
   came in & told their mother the knot had been tied.
(Note: the following marriages were written on the margins of the
   page):
July 12, 1947, Ruth Murph & William Leckie Mattox, Jr. were married
   5 o'clock at home. Rev. C. E. Means performed the ceremony in
   presence of quite a large gathering.
John Speight Murph Married Frances Jones in Kinston, N. C. May 10
   1947.
Marion Frances Murph born July 27, 1948.
Mollie Irene Murph & Opie Lee Shelton were Married at Home in
   Marshallville Sept. 29, 1940, 6 P.M.

DEATHS:
Jane Williams Rambo, wife of Danl Rambo, died July 2nd 1838, aged
   yrs., 6 mo., 26 days.
Christian Creswell Rambo son of Danl & Jane W. Rambo died November
   15th 1831.
Jane Rambo, daughter of Danl & Jane W. Rambo died June 26th 1835.
Thirza Lavinia McQueen daughter of Danl & Jane W. Rambo (died)
   September 28th 1837.
Wesley Rambo son of Danl & Jane W. Rambo died 1835.
Daniel Rambo died Thursday September 19th 1861   4:30 o'clock P.M.
   (Age illegible).
Fielding Rambo died August 12th 1881 (or 1887).
Marcellus Rambo died May 7th 1883.
Mary F. Shehee died 20th May 1890   12 o'clock.
John deGraffenried died (of cholera) December 21st 1852,
   55 years, 5 mo., 22 days.
Ann deGraffenried wife of John deGraffenried died (suddenly)
   January 17th 1840.
Joseph Treyvant son of Jno. & Nancy deG. died 28th Oct. 1825.
Henrietta daughter of Jno. & Nancy deG. died Sep. 24th 1831.
Elizabeth A., wife of Geo C. deGraffenried died March 21/55.
(Continued).

RAMBO Bible continued:
Emma Lula daughter of S. F. & A. R. deGraffenried died
    Oct. 4th 1864 Tuesday 9 o'clock 10 min P.M.
Capt. Hopson deGraffenried son of Jno & Nancy deG. was killed at
    battle of Petersburg, Va.
S. F. deGraffenried son of Jno & Nancy deG. died   , he
    was killed by railroad accident near Albany, Ga.
Christopher Tescharner Rambo son of Drury & Regina Rambo died
    Friday March 22nd, 1855 - 11 o'c A.M. Aged 4 years, 7 mo.,
    13 days.
Drury Baker Rambo son of Drury & Regina Rambo died Friday Oct. 10th
    11 o'clock A.M. 1862   congestion. Ages 10 y, 7 m, 7 days.
Mary Hobson Rambo daughter of Drury & Regina Rambo died friday May
    22nd 1863   9 o'c A.M. died of fever. aged 5 y, 5 m, 12 days.
Laurence Wesley Rambo son of Drury & Regina Rambo died November 20th
    1869, Sunday 9:30 o'clock P.M. Billious fever - ages 10 y,
    00 m, 18 days.
Regina H. Rambo died Jan. 15th 1877 - died pneumonia, Aged 23 years,
    3 m. 11 days.
Anna E. Rambo died Feb. 13, 1927 of paralysis in Jackson, Ga. Sick
    only a week or ten days, buried in family lot Bluffton, Ga.,
    Aged 78 yrs, 7 m. 1 d.
Jane Olivia Rambo died 1:15 A.M. Saturday July 23, 1938 at home
    of J. E. Murph. She was buried that day in the Nixon lot by
    the grave of Uncle John Parker in Marshallville, Ga. Aged 82
    yrs, 11 m. 23 d.
Drury deG. Rambo died Jan. 27, 1941 in Marshallville, son of Drury
    & Lillian Nixon Rambo. Buried in the Nixon Cemetery lot.
Regina Rambo wife of Drury Rambo died (of Typhoid fever) June 16th
    1886 - 12:30 P.M. Aged 59 yrs, 5 mo 16 d.
Drury Rambo husband of Regina Rambo died (of LaGrippe) at 10 o'clock
    P.M. on 9th January (friday) 1891, Aged 66 yrs. & 8 mo.
Drury deGraffenried Rambo (son of Drury & Regina Rambo) died Aug.
    8th 1898 at sun-rise with hemorage Jaundice (in the opinion of
    JDR) aged 35 years 8 (or 10) mos & 14 days.
Mollie McCaskill Rambo, wife of J. D. Rambo, died March 7, 1906.
J. D. Rambo died of Paralysis Monday night Jan. 15, 1912 at 8:25
    o'clock. Striken Monday morning at 11:30 in back yard alone.
    Aged 66 yrs, 1 mo. 18 Days.
Laurence McCaskill Rambo, son of Mollie & J. D. Rambo, died Mar.
    5, 1920 at his home in Blakely, Ga.
J. D. Rambo, son of Drury & Lillian Rambo, died at his home in
    Ingleside, Macon, Ga. March 27, 1934. He is buried in the
    Nixon lot at Marshallville, Ga.
Lila H. Rambo, wife of Laurence McG. Rambo was found dead in bed
    about 9 o'clock Sunday A.M. at her home near Bluffton, Ga.,
    Jan. 14, 1940.
Willie Vida Murph died Sept. 17, 1960. Buried in Marshallville,
    Georgia.

SIMS Family Bible
The Bible is in the possession of Mrs. Vadie Sims Johns - daughter
    of Jacob Sims. Bible Published 1886 by American Bible Society.
BIRTHS:
Jacob Sims was born March 14, 1854.
    (Continued).

Sims Family Bible continued:
A. C. Sims was born October 19th, 1857

MARRIAGE:
Jacob Sims & Dolley Cooper was married Nov. 27, 1878

BIRTHS:
Jasin was born Feb. 12, 1899
Lawrence Foster Sims born Nov. 6, 1879
Charles Sims was born July 31, 1881
Lavada Sims was born Feb. 14, 1884
Robert Cleveland Sims was born Dec. 22, 1885
Infant Son born on the 9th day of August 1890
Dollie Sims was born Oct. 1894 - died May 6, 1924
Luleas Sims was born Feb 3, 1897

DEATHS
Jacob Sims died January 13, 1918
Eldridge Sims died Dec. 13, 1893
Martha (Robbins) Sims died February 18, 1906.
Infant son of Mr. & Mrs. Sims died 3 mos. after birth
Vesney Clyde was born June 26, 1895
Lula May Sims was born Feb. 3, 1897
Robert Sims died Nov. 14, 1906

LOWMAN Bible
Owned by Mrs. Fodie Cooper, Dozier, Ala.
Published by N. Y. American Bible Society - 1856

BIRTHS:
Malachi Lowman was born in year 1820 on 17th day of January
Martha Wyse Lowman born 1820 20th Jan
R. Ruby Lowman   born 182- 30th December
R. Lorer Loman was born 1856 on 20th December
Sally Loman was born in the year 1859 Dec 13
Rebecca Lowman B ca 1860 (Supplied by Mrs. Cooper - not in Bible)
M. H. Lowman B. 1862 Sept. (From Mrs. Cooper - not in Bible).
L. A. Lowman Born 1843 13th March
P. F. Lowman Born 1844 on the 4th of August
J. W. E. Lowman was born in yr 1847 on 14th November
M. J. Lowman was born in yr 1849 on the 16th of July
Ben L. Lowman was born in yr 1852 on the 19th of September

DEATHS
M. Lowman departed this life on the 20th of June 1862

MARRIAGES:
Jno. T. Lowman and M. C. Rowell were joined in wedlock
    April 28, 1867
M. Parrish & M. J. Lowman m. July 15, 1816

REV. JESSE W. CORBITT Bible
Owned by Mrs. Wm. M. Quick, Eufaula, Ala.
Published by American Bible Society, New York - MDCCCXVI

MARRIAGES:
Jesse W. Corbitt and his wife Mary McKinnon was Married the 20 of
    (Continued).

January in the year of our lord 1820 By the Rev. James Jenkins.

Daniel E. Corbitt and his wife Martha Jinins was Married March 26 in the year of our lord 1848 By the Rev. Sinclar Limbacer.

Briton Scircey and his wife Christian A. Corbitt was Married March 20 in the year of our Lord 1845 By the Rev. James Shanses.

J. J. Clark and his wife Margaret E. Corbitt was married the 10 of December in the year of our lord 1865 by the Rev. William S. Norton.

Dr. James Reynolds and his wife Leonie E. Clark was married the 2 of September in the year of our Lord 1888 By the Rev. G.(?) F. Betts.

BIRTHS:

Daniel E. Corbitt was bornd the 4 of March in the year of our lord 1822 - Monday 12 o c (Note: o'clock).

Larken J. Corbitt was borned the 22 of May in the year of our Lord 1824 - Sunday 4 o c

Christian A. Corbitt was Borned January 28 in the year of our lord 1827 - Sunday at 11

William S. Corbitt was bornd December 29 in the year of our lord 1829 - Tuesday at 4 o c

Mary F. Corbitt was Bornd August 18 in the year of our lord 1832 - Saturday 11

Jesse A. Corbitt was Bornd April 14 in the year of our lord 1835 - Tuesday 4 ocl

Josephine R. Corbitt was Bornd June 29 in the year of Our lord 1838 - friday night 12 o cl

John W. T. Corbitt was borned September 14 in the year of (our) lord 1841 - tuesday evni (?) 4 o c

Margaret El. Corbitt was Borned February 12 in the year of our lord 1844 - Monday evni 1 oc

Joseph Calaway Searcy was Bornd February the 8 in the year of our Lord 1846 - Sunday

Daniel James Searcy was Borned February 3rd in the year of our Lord 1848 - Thirsday

Mary Amandia Corbitt was Bornd January 22(?) in the year of our Lord 1849 - Monday

Margaret Josephine Corbitt was bornd July 3(?) in year of our Lord 1850 - Wednesday

John C. Scearcy was bornd August 5 in the year of our Lord 1850 - Saturday

Jesse B. Scearcy was bornd October 28 in the year of our Lord 1852 - Thursday

Christian I. J. Corbitt was bornd April 14 in the year of our Lord 1852 - Thursday

Walter J. Clark was bornd September 28 in the year of our Lord 188- (1886?).

Leona E. Clark was bornd Sept. 19 the year of our Lord 1866.

(Torn) Clark was bornd January(?) 29 in the year of our Lord 18--.

Jessie A. Clark was born April 19 in the year of our Lord 1871.

Willie E. Clark was bornd March 18 in the year of our Lord 1873.

Mattie L. Clarke was bornd August 12 in the year of our Lord 1877.

Emma E. Clark was bornd May 12 in the year of our Lord 1881.

Verna Y.(?) Clarke was borned September 18 in the year of our Lord 188-.

TURNIPSEED Bible
Owned by Mrs. William M. Quick, Eufaula, Alabama.
Published by William Flint & Co., Philadelphia, Pa., Cincinnati, O
   Atlanta, Ga., Springfield, Mass. - 1872

MARRIAGES:
This is to Certify that the Rite of Holy Matrimony was Celebrated
   between David C. Turnipseed of Bullock Co., Ala. and Orlenia
   E. Owen of Bullock Co., Ala. on 19th Day of Dec. 1877 at Mrs.
   M. F. Owen's by Rev. W. S. Turner an ordained minister of the
   M. E. Church South. Witness: J. F. Culver & W. A. Owen.
Nathaniel G. Owen & Mary Fletcher Tally were married Dec. 12 1843
D. J. McLeod & Emma E. Owen were married July 7th 1868.
William A. Owen & Ida Tenaresee Borum were married Dec. 4th 1877
Walter Green Owen & Sarah R. Solomon were married Aug. 8th 1888.
David C. Turnipseed & Emma Lilian Scarbrough were married
   Dec. 22, 1896.
David Columbus Turnipseed and Juno Harter Robeson August 9" 1911
   Entered the holy bonds of wedlock at Cleveland Ohio Charles
   Gallemore & O. Badgley Methodist ministers Cleveland Ohio.

BIRTHS:
David Columbus Turnipseed was born April 26th 1846.
Orlenia Elizabeth Turnipseed was born January 8th 1849.
John William Marvin Turnipseed was born December 19th 1878
David Columbus Turnipseed was born July 14, 1880
Walter Felix Turnipseed born Oct. 21 1881.
William Owen Turnipseed was born April 11th 1884
Fletcher Talley Turnipseed was born April 25 1886
Henry Felix Turnipseed was born April 6th 1849.
Clarence Lee Turnipseed was born October 20 1884
Robert Lee Turnipseed was born Nov. 4, 1897.
Lenah Edith Turnipseed was born Dec. 16, 1898 on Friday
Lillian Orlenia Turnipseed was born July 19, 1900 on Thursday
Albert Bowen Turnipseed born Dec. 29 - 1901 Sunday
Mary Ellen and Ida Edna Turnipseed born Aug. 29 - 1904 Sunday
Louise Turnipseed born June 10 1908 Wednesday morning
Emma Lillian Scarbrough born June 30 - 1871
Clarence Augustus Owen born Jan. 17th 1879
John Goun McLeod was born Oct. 16th 1869
Charles J. McLeod was born June 28th 1875
Annie Bell McLeod was born Feb. 3rd 1878.

DEATHS:
John Goun McLeod departed this life June 26th 1878
John William Marvin Turnipseed departed this life June 26th, 187
   age 6 months and 7 days
Nathiel G. Owen departed this life Oct 16th 1864
Mary Fletcher Owen departed this life Aug the 4th 1881
Henry Felix Turnipseed departed this life December 29th 1894
William Turnipseed departed this life Jany 24th 1891
My beloved Sister Ann Batie Owen departed this life
   October 21th 1895
My beloved mother Orlenia Elizabeth Turnipseed departed this
   life Nov. 22th 1895
Robert Lee Turnipseed died Nov. 6 1897
Lenna Edith Turnipseed died Nov. 13 - 1900.
   (Continued).

TURNIPSEED Bible continued:
Clever(?) Scarbrough died Dec. 7 - 1902 - age 17 years
Emma Lillian Turnipseed Died Aug 8 1910 "Rest Dearest One"
Sweet little Lena Corine Owen departed this life Sept. 3rd 1894 -
    age 6 months & 28 days.
Walter Felix Turnipseed died Feb. 19 1936
Foy Reynolds Turnipseed died Oct. 21, 1968.
Dr. Walter Felix Turnipseed died Feb. 19th 1936, Eufaula, Ala.,
    buried at Brundidge, Ala. in the Reynolds family lot.

FAMILY HISTORY:
David Columbus Turnipseed, Jr. was Baptized by Rev. D. C. Crook
    Oct the 2nd 1880
Walter Felix Turnipseed was Baptized by Rev. W. M. Motley(?)
    April the 29th 1882
William Owen Turnipseed was Baptized by Rev. J. L. Skipper
    March 15th 1885.
Fletcher Talley was Baptized by Rev. H. Urquhart July 16th 1860.
Lummie (D. C. Turnipseed, Jr) Joined the church Oct. 2nd
    (Sunday) 1892
Walter joined M. E. Church South October 2nd 1892
William Owen Turnipseed joined the church Sept. 1894.
Fletcher Talley Turnipseed joined the church Sept. 1894.

ALEXANDER McKAY Bible
Publisher: William Flint & Son - 1873

MARRIAGES:
Marriage certificate of Alexander McKay of Barbour Co., Ala. and
    Mary C. Douglass of Barbour Co., Ala., on the 6th of May 1872
    near Louisville, Ala., by Rev. F. L. B. Shaver. Witness:
    C. McKay   A. G.(?) Douglas
Minnie Douglas McKay was married to Julius D. Schaub Wednesday
    evening November Eleventh 1896 at the Presbyterian Church
    in Eufaula, Ala., by the Rev. D. N. Yarbro
Edwin McKay and Julia Massey were married Wednesday Dec. 22, 1897
    at the Baptist Church in Eufaula, Ala., by Rev. Mr. Lipscomb.
Annabel McKay was married to Clarence A. Worrall Saturday February
    Eleventh 1905 at home in Ashville North Carolina.
Nora McKay was married to Samuel D. McCarroll Wednesday Evening
    November twenty eight 1906, at home in Eufaula, Ala.

BIRTHS:
Edwin McKay was born in Barbour County near Louisville, Ala.,
    on 11th of April 1873.
Minnie Douglas McKay born in Barbour County near Louisville, Ala.,
    on 12th of August 1875.
Annie Belle McKay was born in Barbour County near Louisville,
    Ala., on 17th Nov. 1877.
Corrie McKay was born in Barbour County near Louisville, Ala.,
    on 17th day of May 1880
John C. McKay was born in Barbour County near Louisville, Ala.,
    on 17th January 1883.
Nora McKay was born in Clayton Alabama on 19th day of April 1886.
    (Continued)

ALEXANDER McKAY Bible continued:

DEATHS:
John C. McKay Died on the 12 day of January 1886 in Clayton, Ala.
Alexander McKay died on the 9th day of April 1902 in Eufaula, Ala.
Mary C. McKay died on the ___ day of 1937 in Eufaula, Ala.
Minnie McKay Schaub died on the 27th day of June 1955 in Eufaula, Alabama.
Julius Denie Schaub died on the 26 day of September 1956 in Eufaula, Alabama
Edwin McKay died on the ___ day of ___ 1937 in Ashville, N. C.
Nora McKay McCarroll died on the ___ day of ___ in _____.
Corrie McKay died on the 26th day of December 1953 in Eufaula, Alabama.

IMPORTANCE EVENTS:
Mary Denie Schaub was born in Eufaula, Ala., Oct. 2, 1897
Julia McKay born in Ashville N. C. Nov. 15, 1898
Julius Douglas Schaub was born July 3rd 1899 in Eufaula, Ala.
Alexander McKay was born in Eufaula, Ala., Dec. 9th 1902
Samuel Alexander McCarroll was born in Longview, Texas on March 6 1907.

CADE Bible
Owned by Mr. Dozier Cade, Sr., Eufaula, Ala.

On front page: We moved to Eufaula, Ala, 1898
Mrs. J. S. Cade, Eufaula, Ala.
This Bible was Bought in 1877.

MARRIAGES:
James S. Cade of Barbour Co., Ala. and Joanna Smart of Barbour Co. Ala. on May 16th 1877 at Barbour Co., Ala. by Rev. W. H. Patterson. Witness: Thomas Weattey (?) and J. J. Cade.
James S. Cade of Barbour Co. and Carrie E. Martin of Barbour Co. was Married on May 16th 1882.
Rosa Lee Cade of Eufaula, Ala. and John Wiley Vining of Macon, Ga were married June 12th 1906.
Dozier Cade of Eufaula, Ala. and Love Ellis of Enterprise, Ala. were married Mch. 17, 1907.
Carrie Belle Cade of Eufaula, Ala. and Alva Richard Pursley of Americus, Ga. were married June 14th, 1911.
John Martin Cade of Eufaula and Winnie Davis Wood of Montgomery, Ala. were married June 15, 1913.
James Loyd Cade of Eufaula, Ala. and Rebekah Smith of Eufaula, Al were married Nov. 7th 1932.

BIRTHS:
James S. Cade was born Jan. 20th 1855 (or 1857).
Joanna Smart was born Mar. 11th 1859
Mary Cleopatra Cade was born May 24th 1878
Carrie E. Martin was born Feb. 26th 1862
Rosa Lee Cade was born March 2nd 1888
Dozier Cade was born Aug. 29th 1884
Addie Eliza Cade was born Feb. 25th 1886   James Loyd Cade born Feb
John Martin Cade born March 10 1890   5th   1887
(Continued).

CADE Bible continued:

Carrie Bell Cade born June 14th 1893 (or 1895)
Lula Ruth Cade born Nov. 23th 1896.
George Franklin Cade born Nov. 4th 1898

DEATHS:
Joanna Cade died Jan, 23nd 1881
Joanna Cade died June 4th 1881
Mary Cleopatra Cade died August 28th 1885
Addie Eliza Cade died Oct. 3th 1887
Lula Ruth Cade died Dec. 30th 1886
George Franklin Cade died Jan. 24th 1899
John Wiley Vining died Nov. 12, 1906
James Smith Cade died Nov. 11, 1908
Ellis Martin Cade died Aug. 9, 1914
Carrie Martin Cade died Jan. 27th 1928
Love Ellis Cade died Nov. 20, 1958.

MEMORANDA:

John Wesley Vining born Mch 23, 1907
James Clarence Cade born Aug. 29, 1908
Mildred Elizabeth Cade born July 26th, 1911
Ellis Martin Cade born May 16, 1914 *
Dorothy Wood Cade born Dec. 25, 1914
Dozier Copeland Cade born Sept. 8, 1917
Elsie Elizabeth Cade born Feb. 11, 1919 *
Evelyn Ruth Cade born March 23, 1920
William Horace Cade born July 21, 1922
John Martin Cade, Jr. born Sept. 29, 1926 *
Carolyn Cade born Nov. 29th, 1933 **

*   These are children of John Martin Cade.
** This is child of James Loyd Cade.

(Note: This Bible was the only item saved when the Cade
      home burned).

WILLIAM SAPP Bible

MARRIAGES:
William Sapp of Laurel Hill, Florida, and Laura E. Etheridge of
    Henly, Ala. were married at Laurel Hill on the 21st day of
    November In the year of Our Lord 1908. Jos. L. Clary.
    Witnesses: Jno. L. Richbourg and R. R. Fountain.
(The following marriages taken from another page of the Bible).
Wm. Sapp and Hattie H. Wells Married Nov. 19 1865.
Wm. Sapp and Emely Wells Married Dec 25 1881
Wm. Sapp and Laura E. Etheridge Married Nov. 21 1908

BIRTHS:
Wm. Sapp was Borned Aug 30th 1846
Hattie H. Wells   Apr 2   1845
Jessie M. Sapp   Nov. 10 1866
Laura S. Sapp   June 25 1868
J. T. Sapp   Aug. 25 1869
Edna C Sapp   Nov. 28 1871
(Continued).

WILLIAM SAPP Bible continued:

Rachel H. Sapp (Born) sep 10   1873
Caty Sapp   Nov. 2   1875
H. L. Sapp   Sept 15 1876
J. M. Sapp   Oct 3   1878
Emely Wells   Dec 5   1866
Cassie C Sapp   May 16   1884
Mary M Sapp   July 20 1887
Z L Sapp   Sept 1   1889
Wm. J. Sapp   May 5   1892
Gracie V. Sapp   Feb 27   1894
Noma Sapp   Apr 6   1895
Paul Sapp   March 3 1897

DEATHS:
Hattie H Sapp Died Oct 8 1879
Emely Sapp Died Oct 8 1905
William Sapp died March 19, 1924
Laura S. Hughes died Nov. 18, 1951 8:15 PM
Henry L. Sapp Nov. 26, 1952 at 8:35 PM
Joel T. Sapp Aug. 3, 1955.
Paul S. Sapp   (Incomplete).
Wm J. Sapp Aug-17-1960

Edna C. Clark - (Incomplete).

Adams, 1, 3, 26, 62
Allday, 8, 42, 43
Alston, 11, 12
Andress, 47, 48, 49, 50
Andrew(s), 33, 39
Arnold, 66
Avent, 61
Averette, 34
Avery, 14

Badgley, 70
Bailey, 14
Baldwin, 64, 66
Ballowe, 29, 31
Banister, 49
Barlow, 7, 8
Barnes, 12
Barnett, 13
Barrett, 48
Bass, 52
Baxter, 7
Beach, 27
Beckham, 22
Bell, 31
Belyue (?), 30
Berg, 41
Berry, 21
Betts, 69
Beverette, 56
Bizzell, 58
Black, 4
Blackmon, 10, 19
Blackstock, 34
Blalock, 26
Bland, 5
Bledsoe, 24, 25
Boland, 56
Borum, 70
Bostwick, 66
Bowers, 41, 42
Boylston, 43
Boynton, 55
Brantley, 64, 66
Brantly, 27
Bray, 24
Bridges, 14
Brock, 18
Brown, 16, 33, 34, 46
Burham, 40
Burr, 39
Bush, 38
Byrd, 2, 3

Cade, 5, 72, 73
Calhoun, 6, 51
Canfield, 51

75

Cantrell, 17
Caraway, 45, 46
Cargill, 5
Carpenter, 29
Carriker, 43
Carson, 54
Carter, 3, 4, 5
Cassady, 3
Chambliss, 5
Chester, 29
Childs, 63, 66
Christian, 14, 34, 35, 36
Christler, 20
Clark, 69, 74
Clary, 73
Cliatt, 34
Coats, 44
Cockran, 5
Coggins, 44, 45
Colbert, 14
Cole, 9
Coleman, 34
Colins, 9
Collier, 62, 65
Cooper, 68
Cope, 9
Corbitt, 68, 69
Cosby, 39
Cotten, 11
Cottrell, 42
Couch, 43
Cowart, 65
Cox, 14
Coxe, 41
Craddock, 59
Crawford, 12
Crews, 19
Crocker, 8, 21
Crook, 20, 71
Crumbley, 23
Cullens, 3
Culpepper, 37
Culver, 70
Cunningham, 52

Daniel, 31
Danner, 18
Dantzler, 11
Davenport, 17, 39
David, 14,
Davis, 3, 7, 22, 41, 46
Davison, 47
Deal, 4
Decatur, 37
deGraffenried, 63, 65, 66, 67

Dickey, 17
Dillard, 65
Donaldson, 23
Dorsey, 55
Doss, 51
Douglass, 71
Drake, 12, 20
Dudley, 57
Dunbar, 6, 7
Dunning, 55, 56
Durham, 46

Efurd, 9
Ellis, 11, 72
Ellison, 12
English, 21
Engram, 22, 23
Espy, 56
Etheridge, 73
Ethridge, 58

Faulk, 57, 58
Ferguson, 29
Ferrell, 27
Fields, 5
Fincher, 46
Fleming, 51
Floyd, 24
Folkes, 46
Fort, 63, 65
Fountain, 73
Freeman, 17, 18
Frost, 51

Gallemore, 70
Gamble, 16
Garland, 65
Garrington, 20
Garvin, 42
Gillespie, 66
Gillis, 10
Gilmore, 31, 32
Glenn, 56
Goodson, 50
Goodwin, 14, 15, 16, 62, 66
Goree, 25, 26
Grabin, 7
Graf, 43
Graham, 10, 29
Graves, 26
Gray, 1
Green, 37, 38, 45
Grenee, 45
Griffin, 30
Grimmet, 17
Grimmett, 15, 16

Grove, 26, 27
Grubbs, 7
Guyton, 23

Hall, 36, 58
Ham, 15, 17, 18
Hamby, 16
Hammock, 18
Hardenburgh, 24
Hardwick, 4, 32, 59
Harris, 23, 56
Harrison, 50, 51
Harrod, 9
Hartley, 45
Harvey, 40
Harwell, 12, 13
Hattaway, 63, 64, 65, 66
Haygood, 59
Hearn, 25, 28
Heintzelman, 34
Helms, 4
Helton, 34
Henderson, 30
Henkle, 32
Henley, 12
Henry, 17
Herbert, 51
Herndon, 59
Herring, 9
Hester, 51
Hightower, 56
Hill, 12, 52, 53, 65
Hillman, 55
Hinton, 43
Hogan, 26
Holmes, 32, 33
Hooper, 7, 43
Horne, 40
Howell, 6
Hudson, 29
Hughes, 74
Hunt, 13
Hunter, 28

Jackson, 21, 22, 62
Jenkins, 69
Jinins, 69
Johns, 9, 67
Johnson, 6, 7, 8, 9, 10, 11, 38
Jones, 7, 66

Keefer, 41
Keils, 22
Kent, 19
Kerr, 29
Kesseler, 21

Ketcham, 19
Key, 55
Killingworth, 11
King, 6, 7, 9, 37
Kirklin, 66
Kissington, 5

Lambright, 39
Landford, 23
Lane, 53
Lanier, 46
Lawhon, 35
Lee. 11, 16
Lehan, 43
Lesueur, 40
Lewis, 9, 56, 57
Light, 26
Limbacer, 69
Lipscomb, 71
Locke, 21, 22, 23
Lott, 18
Lowe, 29, 55
Lowman, 68
Lunday, 65
Lunsford, 7

Maddox, 14
Mangum, 21
Mann, 7
Maples, 61
Marlon, 43
Martin, 9, 14, 34, 36, 72
Massey, 71
Matheson, 12
Mathews, 17
Mathis, 60
Matthews, 29
Mattox, 61 66
May, 60, 61
McAndrews, 30
McCarroll, 71
McCaskill, 63, 65
McCorkle, 45
McCormick, 43
McCoy, 47
McDonald, 41, 54
McElven, 64, 65
McFarlane, 39
McIntosh, 22
McKay, 71
McKenney, 34
McKenzie, 40, 41, 50, 51
McKinnon, 68
McKinzie, 50
McLean, 4, 57, 58
McLendon, 18, 60, 61

McLeod, 6, 7, 20, 29, 70
McLeroy, 5
McQueen, 49, 65
McRae, 7, 15
McReynolds, 1
Means, 66
Miller, 28, 55
Minton, 51
Montgomery, 51, 52, 53
More, 11
Moore, 12
Morris, 5
Morrison, 28
Mosly, 49
Motley, 28, 29, 30, 31, 71
Murph, 62, 64, 65, 66, 67
Murphy, 16

Nason, 56
Nettles, 47
Newell, 44
Nixon, 64, 65
Norman, 17
Norton, 7, 9, 69
Norwood, 57, 58, 59

O'Conner, 58
Oliver, 37, 38
Ott, 11
Owens, 59, 70

Parish, 14
Parker, 4
Parmer, 19, 46
Parrish, 68
Pate, 41
Patterson, 72
Peeples, 55
Perry, 28
Peterson, 43
Phelps, 37
Philips, 3, 4
Phillips, 18, 39
Pickett, 23
Pinkston, 54
Pitman, 4
Pollard, 49
Posey, 3, 4
Powell, 1, 38, 61
Preston, 19
Pringle, 47
Pursley, 72
Pyle, 61

Rambo, 61, 62, 63, 64, 65, 66, 67
Ramsey, 15
Randolph, 66

77

Rawlinson, 26
Rawls, 27
Reese, 26
Reeves, 22
Rembert, 21
Reynolds, 69
Rhames, 49
Richard, 23
Richards, 3, 5, 59
Richardson, 1
Richbourg, 73
Rivers, 13
Roberson, 36
Roberts, 27, 32, 40
Robeson, 70
Rogers, 38
Rose, 6, 7
Ross, 57
Rouse, 23
Rowell, 68
Rown, 22
Rudolph, 65
Rush, 30

Sale, 23, 26
Sapp, 73, 74
Sartor, 62
Sasser, 45
Scarbrough, 70, 71
Schaub, 71
Scircey, 69
Scott, 44
Screws, 20
Searcy, 3, 59, 69
See (Lee?), 12
Session, 31
Sewell, 17
Shanses, 69
Shaver, 71
Shaw, 51
Shehee, 65
Shelton, 51, 66
Shields, 12, 13
Shirling, 51
Sidnor, 40
Simonton, 60
Sims, 49, 56, 67
Skipper, 32, 33, 71
Slaughter, 17
Smart, 72
Smith, 1, 26, 28, 31, 34, 72
Snead, 51, 52
Snipes, 52, 53
Solomon, 70
Speir, 26

Spencer, 39, 40
Sperlin, 31
Spigener, 26
Spratling, 13, 14, 35
Spurlin, 43, 44
Stafford, 65
Stanton, 6
Stephens, 57, 58
Stewart, 33, 52
Stow, 27
Stroud, 26, 27
Stuart, 59
Stuckey, 20, 46
Sutton, 41
Sweeny, 43
Sylvester, 20, 21, 22, 23, 52, 53

Talley, 28
Tally, 70
Tanner, 15
Taylor, 8, 19, 21, 35, 38
Teal, 19
Teat, 37
Templeton, 17, 18
Tew, 46, 47
Thomas, 8, 42, 43
Thomley, 46
Thompson, 14, 30, 42
Thornton, 21, 22
Till, 15
Toney, 52
Trammell, 33, 34
Trent, 33, 34
Tully, 8, 42, 43
Turman, 56
Turner, 17, 18, 41, 70
Turnipseed, 5, 30, 70, 71
Tye, 5
Tyson, 37

Urquhart, 71

Vaughn, 12
Veal, 36, 37
Vickery, 5
Vining, 5, 72, 73

Waddell, 59
Wandland, 43
Wadsworth, 30
Walker, 14, 15, 28, 30
Walters, 40
Watkins, 21, 63, 65
Watson, 6, 7, 20, 38
Weattey (?), 72
Wells, 24, 43, 73, 74

West, 51
Westbrook, 40
Wharton, 42
Wheeler, 4
White, 51
Whittington, 54
Whittle, 55
Wiggins, 8
Wilkerson, 19
Williams, 10, 15, 64
Wilson, 1, 28, 51, 52
Windle, 30
Winn, 12
Wiseman, 17
Wood, 2, 3, 4, 5, 6, 72
Woodham, 52
Woods, 22, 58
Wooten, 65
Worrall, 71
Wright, 39, 40

Yadon, 20
Yarbro, 71
Young, 7

www.ingramcontent.com/pod-product-compliance
Lightning Source LLC
Chambersburg PA
CBHW020702300426
44112CB00007B/483